317-1
87

# God's Presence in History

the text of this book is printed
on 100% recycled paper

*The Deems Lectures*

The Reverend Charles Force Deems, born in 1820, was deeply concerned with the relationship of science and philosophy to religion. In 1881 he founded the American Institute of Christian Philosophy for the investigation of the most significant questions pertaining to this relationship. In 1895, two years after the death of Dr. Deems, the American Institute of Christian Philosophy endowed a lectureship of philosophy at New York University in his honor and for a continuation of the purpose for which the Institute had been founded.

Dr. Fackenheim's lectures were sponsored by the Deems Fund, and were delivered in 1968. Other Deems lectures published by New York University Press are:

*Faith and Speculation* by Austin M. Farrar,

*The Logic of Religion* by Joseph M. Bochenski, O.P., and

*The Christian Existentialist* by Bernard Häring, C.Ss.R.

# God's Presence in History:
## *Jewish Affirmations and Philosophical Reflections*

Containing the Charles F. Deems Lectures
delivered at New York University in 1968

*by Emil L. Fackenheim*

*HARPER TORCHBOOKS*
*Harper & Row, Publishers*
*New York, Hagerstown, San Francisco, London*

A hardcover edition of this book was originally published by New York University Press.


GOD'S PRESENCE IN HISTORY

Copyright © 1970 by New York University

First HARPER TORCHBOOK edition published 1972

ISBN: 0-06-131690-3
78 79 80 81 82 10 9 8 7 6 5

# Preface

The nucleus of the 1968 Charles F. Deems Lectures here offered in print was a paper given in 1967 to the members of the I. Meier Segals Center for the Study and Advancement of Judaism. I owe incalculable inspiration to the members of the Center, who have been meeting for a week in the summer for the past four years. While I cannot mention my debt to individuals I must make two exceptions. The influence of Elie Wiesel (to whom this small volume is dedicated) will be obvious to any reader: his writings are forcing Jewish theological thought in our time into a new dimension. For my concept of "root experience" I owe a fundamental debt to Irving Greenberg's concept of "orienting experience": his stubbornly historical thinking has liberated me from some false philosophical abstractions.

Much has had to remain unsaid in this small book, and not because of its smallness alone. Of this I will here only say that despite their apparently loose form the three chapters are not lacking in method. Each follows the methodological requirements of its subject matter. The method of the first chapter may be described as combining phenomenological and historical elements, containing the one because what is sought is a structured essence and not sheer historical fact, and the other because this essence is vulnerable to epoch-making events. The method of the second chapter is that of a philosophico-theological encounter whose goal remains limited to the discovery of compatibilities. The method of the third chapter is neo-Midrashic (as that term is defined in the first chapter), and its standpoint is immediacy after reflection (as that term is defined in the second chapter). In the first two chapters

v

religious commitment remains ultimately suspended, respectively by phenomenologico-historical and philosophical detachment. The reader unconcerned with purely philosophical questions may wish to proceed from the first straightaway to the last chapter, in which all detachment is swept aside.

Toronto, February 1969.

# Contents

*For Elie Wiesel*

# I     The Structure of Jewish Experience

## *Introduction*

"The heavens were opened," writes the prophet Ezekiel in his opening chapter, "and I saw visions of God" (Ezek. 1:1). These may be common words in certain types of mystical literature which affirm visions of Divinity freely and easily. In the context of the Hebrew Bible (which shrinks from such visions in awe and terror) they are rare and bold. It is therefore not surprising that the chapter which follows these opening words is full of all-but-unintelligible mysteries. According to rabbinic tradition there is not, with the possible exception of Genesis, chapter 1 (which deals with Ma'assey Bereshith—"the Works of the Beginning"), any other chapter in the whole Bible which can match in depth and mysteriousness Ezekiel, chapter 1, which deals with Ma'assey Merkavah ("the Works of the Wheel")—nothing less than the nature of Divinity itself. No wonder the rabbis considered it dangerous for all except the most pious and learned to try to fathom the secrets of that chapter.

Yet the same tradition which holds this view also seems

deliberately and dramatically to contradict it. In a well-known Midrash it is asserted that what Ezekiel once saw in heaven was far less than what all of Israel once saw on earth. Ezekiel, and indeed all the other prophets, did not see God but only visions and similes of God; they were like men who perceive a king of flesh and blood surrounded by servants of flesh and blood, and who are forced to ask, "which one is the king?" In the sharpest possible contrast, the Israelites at the Red Sea had no need to ask which one was the King: "As soon as they saw Him, they recognized Him, and they all opened their mouths and said, "This is my God, and I will glorify Him'" (Exod. 15:2). Even the lowliest maidservant at the Red Sea saw what Isaiah, Ezekiel, and all the other prophets never saw.[1]

The Midrash just cited and paraphrased deals with the subject of this discourse—God's presence in history. This subject is dealt with in countless passages in Jewish and Christian literature. The cited Midrash has special significance, however, because it affirms God's presence in history in full awareness of the fact that the affirmation is strange, extraordinary, or even paradoxical. The God of Israel is no mythological deity which mingles freely with men in history. He is beyond man— so infinitely beyond human reach that an opening of the heavens themselves is required if He is to become humanly accessible. Few are the men to whom such an opening was ever granted, and the reports of these few are so obscure as to be unintelligible to nearly all others. So infinitely is the Divine above the human! Nevertheless, the Midrash insists that not messengers, not angels, not intermediaries, but God Himself acts in human history—and He was unmistakably present to a whole people at least once.

The ancient Midrash affirms God's presence in history. Modern man on his part seems compelled to deny it. Philosophers in any case are inclined to do so and have in fact demythologized history ever since they cleared it of the Homeric gods. In the modern world, moreover, theologians have been prone to follow the philosophical example. How can there be "supernatural" incursions into "natural" history? How can historical explanation come to an arbitrary halt in order to accept the Inexplicable—the presence of God? God, it seems, must be expelled from history by the modern historian, just as He is expelled from nature by the modern scientist. And the modern Jewish and Christian theologian cannot affirm God's presence in history but at most only His providence over it—a providence caused by a God who may somehow use nature and man in history, but who is Himself absent from history.

Moreover, even this weakened doctrine still remains with insuperable difficulties. How can divine Providence rule over history and yet allow human freedom within it? And how can one believe in a providential history and still take seriously the vast evil which occurs in it? So grave are these difficulties that the bolder and more radical among modern theologians have been led to revolutionize traditional doctrines. There is no externally superintending divine Providence, compelling human freedom and using evil for its own good purposes. Divine Providence is immanent in human freedom and consists of its progressive realization. Meaning in history lies in its forward direction—one in which human freedom raises itself ever higher toward Divinity, and evil comes ever closer to being conquered. There is either this kind of meaning in history, or else there is no meaning in it at all.[2]

Such were the responses of eighteenth- and nineteenth-century theological thought to modern intellectual difficulties. Far more radical responses seem forced upon twentieth-century theological thought by what are no mere intellectual difficulties but rather historical upheavals and catastrophes. As decent and sober a thinker as Immanuel Kant could still seriously believe that war served the purposes of Providence.[3] After Hiroshima, all war is known to be at best a necessary evil. As saintly a theologian as St. Thomas Aquinas could in all seriousness argue that tyrants serve providential ends, for if it were not for tyrants there would be no opportunity for martyrdom.[4] After Auschwitz, anyone using this argument would be guilty of blasphemy. Indeed, Hiroshima and Auschwitz seem to have destroyed any kind of Providence—the newer, immanent kind no less than the older, externally superintending kind. After these dread events, occurring in the heart of the modern, enlightened, technological world, can one still believe in the God who is necessary Progress any more than in the God who manifests His Power in the form of a superintending Providence? It seems that anyone who today still seeks the Divine at all must totally contradict the ancient Midrash and turn away from history in his search for God—whether to Eternity above history, to nature below it, or to an individualistic inwardness divorced from it.

The trauma of contemporary events affects all religious belief. It is Jewish religious belief, however, which is most traumatically affected. The Jewish people were first to affirm the God of history. They have had a unique relation to this God, if only, in their case alone and for nearly four millennia, because collective survival itself was bound up with Him. Yet today it seems that whereas other believers have reason to reject the God of history, a Jew has nothing less than an obligation. At Auschwitz, Jews were murdered, not because they had disobeyed the God of history, but rather because their great-grandparents had obeyed Him.[5] They had done so by raising Jewish children. Dare a Jew of today continue to obey the God of history—and thus expose to the danger of a second Auschwitz, himself, his children, and his children's children? Never, within or without Jewish history, have men anywhere had such a dreadful, such a horrifying, reason for turning their backs on the God of history.

And yet, before taking this step, unprecedented in four thousand years of Jewish faith, a Jewish believer must pause, and pause at length. Throughout all her existence Israel has stayed with the God of history; throughout all her existence this God of history—or, at any rate, Jewish faith in Him—has kept Israel as well. Is it likely that rational criticism alone suffices to destroy this faith when Jewish history has been rich in rational thinkers? Is it obvious without further analysis that even the catastrophes of our age are by themselves sufficient to dispose of this God when Jewish faith has survived many prior tragedies? Clearly, before judging or rejecting the Jewish faith, we must give it a serious hearing.

Even a preliminary hearing is enough to destroy rash answers. While Auschwitz is new, evil in history is not. Thus Jeremiah protests against the prosperity of the wicked (Jer. 12:1)—and receives no answer. Job protests against his own undeserved suffering—and what God says in response "does not answer the charge; it does not even touch upon it."[6] To give still a third example, when Jerusalem was destroyed by the Romans the rabbis could see no meaning in the event. Yet in all three cases—and in countless others—Jewish faith not only refused to despair of God, it also refused to disconnect Him with history and to seek escape in mysticism or other-worldliness.

In order to see that this was no blind stubbornness, unaware of the possibility of religious alternatives, we need not go beyond the Midrash which we have already cited. The Midrashic author is not unaware of the possibility of a religious flight from history. On the contrary, he first refers to Ezekiel's vision —the Biblical chapter which, more than any other, has encouraged otherworldly mysticism within Judaism—and then exalts what the maidservants saw *within* history above what Ezekiel saw *beyond* it. Moreover—as if to anticipate the objection that such a God is a mere tribal god to be abandoned as religion advances toward universalism—he goes on to add boldly and paradoxically that He who at the Red Sea fought on Israel's behalf was none other than the Creator of the World.[7]

Clearly, then, in dealing with the ancient Jewish faith in God's presence in history we must ask new and unprecedented questions in our time. But, no less clearly, we cannot ask these questions until we have understood that faith. To achieve such an understanding will be the task of our first chapter.

But it may well seem that to begin with this topic is to

miss the announced title of this book. We begin with a particular subject—the Jewish faith in God's presence in history. The announced title, however, is a universal one—God's presence in history—and it may appear that this subject calls for concepts of God-in-general, history-in-general, Providence-in-general, and their acceptability to modern-man-in-general. This, however, would be a false start. If God is ever present in history, this is not a presence-in-general but rather a presence to particular men in particular situations. To be sure, unless it were that of a mere tribal deity, such a presence must have universal implications. These implications, however, are manifest only in the particular; and they make of the men to whom they are manifest, not universalistic philosophers who rise above their situations, but rather witnesses, in, through, and because of their particularity to the nations. In this book, our direct concern is with the destiny of the Jewish faith in the modern world. But inextricably bound up with it is the question of whether, and if so how, it is possible and necessary for the Jew of today to be a witness to the world.[8] Yet for a Jew—today or at any other time—to dissolve the particularity of either his Jewishness or his historical situation into humanity-in-general or history-in-general would not be to rise above a "narrow parochialism" to a "broad universalism." It would be a betrayal of his post.[9]

## Root Experiences

It would be incongruous for us to reject, as misleading, any beginning with abstract notions of history-in-general, and yet ourselves begin with Jewish history-in-general. We must rather begin with particular events within the history of the Jewish faith, or, more precisely, with epoch-making events.

Even this term is not yet precise or radical enough. In its millennial career the Jewish faith has passed through many epoch-making events, such as the end of prophecy and the destruction of the first Temple, the Maccabean revolt, the destruction of the second Temple, and the expulsion from Spain. These events each made a new claim upon the Jewish faith and, indeed, would not be epoch-making if it were otherwise. They did not, however, produce a new faith. What occurred instead was a confrontation in which the old faith was tested in the light of contemporary experience. Jewish history abounds with such confrontations between past and present. At least until the rise of the modern world, these have all one common characteristic. The strain of confrontation may often have come near a breaking point, yet present experience, however new, unanticipated, and epoch-making, never destroyed the past faith. Its claims upon the present survived. But—and this is crucial—this past faith had not come from nowhere but had itself originated in historical events. These historical events, therefore, are more than epoch-making. In the context of Judaism, we shall refer to them as root experiences.[10]

What, considered abstractly, are the characteristics of a root experience in Judaism? What are the conditions without which a past event cannot continue to make a present claim— the claim that God is present in history? According to Rabbi Eliezer, the author of the Midrash quoted at the beginning of this chapter, the maidservants at the Red Sea saw what even Ezekiel did not see. This means, on the one hand, that Rabbi Eliezer himself does not see and, on the other hand, that he knows that the maidservants saw, and he does not. If he himself saw, he would not defer to their vision—his own being superior or equal to theirs and in any case a present standard by which to measure the past. If he did not know that they had seen, their past vision would be of no present relevance and, indeed, would be wholly inaccessible. Only because of this dialectical relation between present and past can a past experience legislate to the present. *This is the first condition of a root experience in Judaism.*

By itself, however, this condition (as yet far from fully intelligible)[11] is far from sufficient as well. According to our Midrash, this condition would apply to Ezekiel's vision as much as to the maidservants' at the Red Sea. Yet Ezekiel's vision is not a root experience in Judaism. It is the experience of an isolated individual and may legislate to isolated individuals after him—those few to whom the heavens are accessible. At the Red Sea, however, the whole people saw, the lowly maidservants included, and what occurred before their eyes was not an opening of heaven but a transformation of earth—an historic event affecting decisively all future Jewish generations. These future generations, on their part, do not, like the maidservants at the Red Sea, see the presence of God. But to this day they recall twice daily in their prayers the natural-historical event through which that presence was once manifest, and the Passover Seder is wholly dedicated to it. Indeed, according to some rabbis, so profoundly legislating is this past event to future times that it will continue to be remembered even in the Messianic days.[12] *Its public, historical character is the second condition of a root experience in Judaism.*

Still missing is a third condition, and this will turn out to be the crucial one. The vision of the maidservants at the Red Sea may be analyzed into two components. First, they experienced impending disaster at the hands of the pursuing Egyptian army and then salvation through the division of the Red Sea; that is, they experienced a natural-historical event. But they also experienced the presence of God. Subsequent generations, on their part, recollect the natural-historical event, but they do not see what the maidservants saw. Both points are not in question in the Midrashic account. What is in question is whether, and if so how, *subsequent generations have access to the vision of the maidservants—to the presence of God.*

If they have no such access, then the event at the Red Sea cannot be a root experience in Judaism. A skeptic would in any case deny that the natural-historical event even happened, or else view it as a mere fortunate coincidence. What matters here is that even a believer would have little cause for remembering it. For the "miracle" remembered would be for him, not a past event of divine Presence, but merely one particular effect of a general—and remote—divine Cause. And, if his concern were with the general divine Cause, no particular effect would stand out in importance; and, if it were with particular effects, it should be with *present* effects, not with the dimly remembered past. In connection with a discussion of the religious relevance of history, Hegel somewhere wryly quotes a proverb to the effect that with the passage of time the past loses its truth. If later generations of Jewish believers have no access whatever to the vision of the maidservants, this proverb would be applicable to the event at the Red Sea.

Such proverbs cease to apply, however, if the past vision of the maidservants is somehow still presently accessible; for in that case a divine Presence, manifest in and through the past natural-historical event, could not fail to legislate to future generations. (This is true at least if, as the Midrash states, the Divinity manifest is not a finite, tribal deity but the universal "Creator of the World." The past presence of such a God can continue to legislate even in the Messianic days.) *This accessibility of past to present is the third and final characteristic of a root experience in Judaism.*

This characteristic is clearly if implicitly asserted by Jewish tradition. Thus the pious Jew remembering the Exodus and the salvation at the Red Sea does not call to mind events now dead and gone. He reenacts these events *as a present reality:* only thus is he assured that the past saving God saves still,[13] and that He will finally bring ultimate salvation. We have already stressed that Rabbi Eliezer knows that the maidservants saw the divine Presence at the Red Sea; we must now add that *he could not have this knowledge unless he had somehow himself access to their vision.*

But how shall we understand this access when Rabbi Eliezer—and the pious Jew during the Passover Seder—does not see what the maidservants saw? Indeed, how shall we understand the original event itself—a divine Presence which is manifest *in* and *through* a natural-historical event, not in the heavens beyond it?

An understanding is given in a remarkable passage in Martin Buber's *Moses*—one so remarkable and relevant to our

purpose that we shall return to it again and again throughout
this book. Buber writes:

> What is decisive with respect to the inner history of
> Mankind . . . is that the children of Israel understood
> this as an act of their God, as a "miracle"; which does
> not mean that they interpreted it as a miracle, but that
> they experienced it as such, that as such they perceived
> it. . . .
>
> The concept of miracle which is permissible from the
> historical approach can be defined at its starting point
> as an abiding astonishment. The . . . religious person . . .
> abides in that wonder; no knowledge, no cognition, can
> weaken his astonishment. Any causal explanation only
> deepens the wonder for him. The great turning-points in
> religious history are based on the fact that again and
> ever again an individual and a group attached to him
> wonder and keep on wondering; at a natural phenomeron,
> at an historical event, or at both together; always at some-
> thing which intervenes fatefully in the life of this indi-
> vidual and this group. They sense and experience it as
> a wonder. This, to be sure, is only the starting-point of
> the historical concept of wonder, but it cannot be ex-
> plained away. Miracle is not something "supernatural"
> or "superhistorical," but an incident, an event which can
> be fully included in the objective, scientific nexus of na-
> ture and history; the vital meaning of which, however,
> for the person to whom it occurs, destroys the security
> of the whole nexus of knowledge for him, and explodes
> the fixity of the fields of experience named "Nature" and
> "History." . . .
>
> We may ascribe what gives rise to our astonishment
> to a specific power. . . . For the performance of the
> miracle a particular magical spirit, a special demon, a
> special idol is called into being. It is an idol just because
> it is special. But this is not what historical consideration
> means by miracle. For where a doer is restricted by other
> doers, the current system of cause and effect is replaced
> by another. . . . *The real miracle means that in the as-
> tonishing experience of the event the current system of
> cause and effect becomes, as it were, transparent and*

*permits a glimpse of the sphere in which a sole power,
not restricted by any other, is at work.*[14]

Buber's modern terms may be applied to the ancient Midrash in every particular. First, they remove a false understanding. Second, they make sense of a divine Presence manifest in and through a natural-historical event. Third, they explain how Rabbi Eliezer, while unable to see what the maidservants saw, nevertheless has access to their experience. Let us consider these three points in turn.

Those present at the Red Sea do not *infer* their God from the natural-historical event in an attempt to *explain* that event. A god of this kind would not be "Creator of the world" or "sole Power" but only a "magical spirit." He would not be "immediately recognized" but at most would be a probable hypothesis. And he would not be present but, rather, necessarily absent. As for the abiding astonishment, this would be dissipated by the explanation. This much would be true even of the original witnesses at the Red Sea. As for subsequent believers (who already possess this or some other explanation), they would not be astonished at all. And the past would be a dead past without present relevance. So much for the first point. What of the second?

The "sole Power" is immediately present *at the Red Sea*, in and through *the natural-historical event* for *the abiding astonishment of the witnesses.* All three terms introduced by Buber are needed, and they are intelligible only in their relation. (a) Except for the immediate presence of the sole Power the natural-historical event would not be a miracle but rather a strange incident in need of explanation; and the astonishment would only be curiosity or, in any case, not abide, for it would vanish when the explanation is given. (b) Except for the abiding astonishment, the sole Power would not be present or, in any case, not be *known* to be present; and the miracle would, once again, be a mere incident to be explained. (c) Except for the natural-historical event, the sole Power, if present at all, would either be present in the heavens beyond history, or else dissolve all historical particularity by its presence within it; and the abiding astonishment would be equally historically vacuous. But the salvation at the Red Sea is not historically vacuous. It has "intervene[d] fatefully" in the history, if not of all mankind, certainly of Israel.

To come to the third point, how then is Rabbi Eliezer (and the pious Jew during the Passover Seder) related to the maid-servants at the Red Sea? *In reenacting the natural-historical event, he reenacts the abiding astonishment as well, and makes it his own.* Hence the "sole Power" present then is present still. Hence memory turns into faith and hope. Hence the event at the Red Sea is recalled now and will continue to be recalled even in the Messianic days. Thus the reenacted past legislates to present and future. Thus, in Judaism, it is a root experience.

## Saving and Commanding Divine Presence

We have thus far used one particular root experience in Judaism in an attempt to elicit the characteristics of all such experiences. We must now turn, however briefly, to one other such experience—the commanding Presence at Sinai. Not only is every attempt to understand Judaism without Sinai impossible, it is also the case that, except for a commanding Presence, any divine Presence in history remains, for Jewish experience, at best fragmentary.

The divine Presence thus far considered is a saving Presence. Salvation is not here, however, what it might be in a different religious context. It occurs *within* history, not in an Eternity beyond it, nor for a soul divorced from it, nor as an apocalyptic or Messianic event which consummates history. It therefore points necessarily to *human action.* In the Biblical account Moses cries unto God, but is told to bid his people go forward (Exod. 14:15). The Midrash dwells on this thought and affirms that no salvation would have occurred had Israel shrunk in fear from walking through the divided sea.[15] And it exalts one Naḥshon Ben Amminadab who, in the midst of universal hesitation, was first to jump into the waves.[16] A commanding Voice is heard even as the saving event is seen; and salvation itself is not complete until the Voice is heeded.

The astonishment abides as the commanding Voice is heard: this becomes clear when that Voice comes on the scene in its own right to legislate to future generations—in the root experience of Sinai. The structure of that experience is reflected in the following Midrash:

> Rabbi Azaryiah and Rabbi Aḥa in the name of Rabbi Yoḥanan said: When the Israelites heard at Sinai the word "I" [i.e., the first word of the ten commandments], their souls left them, as it says, "If we hear the voice . . . any more, then we shall die" (Deut. 5:22). . . . The Word then returned to the Holy One, blessed be He and said: "Sovereign of the Universe, Thou art full of life, and Thy law is full of life, and Thou has sent me to the dead, for they are all dead." Thereupon the Holy One, blessed be He, sweetened [i.e., softened] the Word for them. . . .[17]

The Midrash affirms that at Sinai, as at the Red Sea, the whole people saw what Ezekiel and the other prophets never saw.[18] Yet because the divine Presence is here a commanding Presence, the astonishment has a different structure. A commandment effected by a distant divine Cause would be divine only by virtue of its external sanction and inspire no abiding astonishment. If the astonishment abides, it is because Divinity is present in the commandment. Because it is a commanding rather than a saving Presence, however, the abiding astonishment turns into deadly terror. Indeed, such a Presence is, in the first instance, nothing short of paradoxical. For, being commanding, it addresses human freedom. And being sole Power, it destroys that freedom because it is only human. Yet the freedom destroyed is also required.

Hence the divine commanding Presence can be divine, commanding, and present only if it is doubly present; and the human astonishment must be a double astonishment. As sole Power, the divine commanding Presence destroys human freedom; as gracious Power, it restores that freedom, and indeed exalts it, for human freedom is made part of a covenant with Divinity itself. And the human astonishment, which is terror at a Presence at once divine and commanding, turns into a second astonishment, which is joy, at a Grace which restores and exalts human freedom by its commanding Presence.[19]

According to the Midrash all generations of Israel were present at Sinai, and the Torah is given whenever a man receives it.[20] A man can receive it only if he reenacts the double astonishment. If he remains frozen in stark terror, he cannot observe the commandments at all. And, if he evades that terror, he may observe the commandments, but he has lost the divine commanding Presence. Only by reenacting both the terror and the joy can he participate in a life of the commandments which lives before the sole Power and yet is human.

## *Dialectical Contradictions*

But threats arise to the reenactment of the root-experiences of Judaism from two main quarters. One quarter is history itself. Since the reenactment does not occur in an historical vacuum, each historical present, or at any rate each epoch-making historical present, makes its own demands over against the past and its reenactment; and, since each epoch-making present must be taken seriously in its own right, it is not possible to anticipate the outcome. (Threats of this kind will occupy us during the remainder of this book.) Another type of threat, however, may be dealt with at once, for it is general, unchanging, and abstractable from history. This is the threat posed by reflective, philosophical thought.

The root experience itself is an immediacy, and so is its reenactment by subsequent believers. It is the potential object, however, of *philosophical reflection*; and the moment such reflection occurs it reveals the root experience to be shot through with at least three all-pervasive, dialectical contradictions.

The first of these is between divine transcendence and

divine involvement. The "sole Power" present at the Red Sea and Mount Sinai manifests a *transcendent* God, for involvement would limit His Power; it manifests an *involved* God as well if only because it is a Presence. As will be seen, this contradiction exists even in the case of the saving Presence. In the case of the commanding Presence it is unmistakable.

This contradiction is logically first, but no more significant than the other two—respectively, between divine Power and human freedom, and between divine involvement with history and the evil which exists within it.

Divinity would not contradict human freedom if it were either present but finite, or infinite but absent—confined, so to speak, to heaven and leaving to man the undisputed control of earth. An infinite divine Presence, in contrast, is a present sole Power, which "explodes the fixity of nature and history," rendering "transparent" the causal nexus constituting both; and this negates the self and its freedom.

At the same time, the divine Presence *requires* the self and its freedom in the very moment of its presence. There is no abiding astonishment unless men exist who can be astonished; moreover, the divine Presence—saving as well as commanding—remains incomplete unless human astonishment terminates in action. Conceivably Ezekiel's selfhood dissolved in the moment in which the heavens were opened. This is impossible when, as at the Red Sea, salvation occurs to a flesh-and-blood people; or when, as at Sinai, the divine Presence gives commandments over for human performance.

The third contradiction arises because a God revealed as sole Power in one moment of history is revealed, in that very moment, as the God of all history.[21] Above we have rejected, as alien to the dynamic of the Jewish faith, all abstract doctrines concerning God-in-general, Providence-in-general, or man-in-general, which are only accidentally "applied" to the historical particular. It now emerges, however, that universality is implicit *in* the particular. A God present in one historical moment would not be "sole Power" if He were *confined to* that moment. He who fought at the Red Sea on Israel's behalf would not be "Creator of the World" if, having once fought, He could fight no more. Nor could the event of His presence be subsequently reenacted. But, if the God present in one moment of history is the God of all history, He is in conflict with the evil which is within it.

This must be listed as a third contradiction over and above that between divine Power and human freedom, if only because not all evil in history is attributable to human sin; and, still more decisively, because sin cannot be viewed as an act of freedom which, real from a human standpoint, is, from the standpoint of divine Providence, either an unreal shadow or an instrument to its purposes. These views are ruled out by the root experiences of Judaism—by the fact that the divine Presence occurs *within* history, not as its consummation or transfiguration. Salvation at the Red Sea is real only because the prior threat of catastrophe is real; as will be seen, it is incomplete even when it occurs; and—to put it mildly—when in subsequent ages this root experience is reenacted salvation is not always a present reality. Similarly, the freedom to reject the divine commanding Presence at Sinai exists at the very moment of presence, and this Presence cannot, as it were, play games with itself when it allows that possibility; moreover— again to put it mildly—subsequent generations of Israelites have not always matched the faithfulness of the generation of Sinai.

Such are the contradictions in the root experiences of Judaism insofar as they concern our present purpose. Philosophical reflection, on becoming aware of these contradictions, is tempted to remove them, and to do so by means of a retroactive *destruction of the root experiences themselves*. At this point, however, Jewish theological thought exhibits a stubbornness which, soon adopted and rarely if ever abandoned, may be viewed as its defining characteristic. Negatively, this stubbornness consists of resisting all forms of thought which would remove the contradictions of the root experiences of Judaism at the price of destroying them. Positively, it consists of developing logical and literary forms which can preserve the root experiences of Judaism despite their contradictions.

Jewish theological thought resists, first, a God who is sole Power but *without involvement*, withdrawn from history and demanding a like withdrawal from history on the part of His human worshippers. There has always been room for mysticism within Judaism, but never for an otherworldly mysticism which abandons salvation *in* and commandments for history, thus retroactively destroying the events at the Red Sea and Sinai.

Jewish theological thought resists, second, a sole Power which *overwhelms* history, allowing no room for either freedom or evil and manifesting itself as *Fate*. To be sure, it may seem at times that "all is in the hands of Heaven except the fear of Heaven." Even at such times, however, the fear of Heaven, far from a "small thing,"[22] is what makes history to the extent to which human freedom then can make it. To embrace fatalism would be retroactively to destroy the freedom manifest at both Sinai and the Red Sea, and thus these root experiences themselves.

Jewish theological thought resists, finally, any notion of a God who is not, after all, "sole Power" or "Creator of the world"—*a god as finite as the idols*. Such a notion, to be sure, is not rejected simply; i.e., at the price of belittling or denying either human freedom or evil. But neither is it simply acceptable. Instead, a dialectical tension develops, and this points to a future in which evil is vanquished by divine Power and human freedom, and in which divine Power and human freedom are reconciled. This future, a necessity for theological thought, is a necessity for immediate experience as well, and indeed rivals in significance the root experiences of the Red Sea and Sinai. It is not, however, itself a root experience, for it is a future anticipated rather than a past reenacted. If nevertheless it is as basic as these root experiences, it is because, without that anticipation, any reenactment of the root experiences of Judaism remains incomplete. Indeed, these experiences themselves remain incomplete. The Messianic faith arose at a relatively late date in Jewish history. As will be seen, it is implicit in Judaism ever since the Exodus.

## The Midrashic Framework

Negatively, Jewish theological thought resists the dissipation of the root experiences of Judaism. Positively, it aims at preservation. It succeeds in its aim by becoming Midrashic. In the preceding pages we have already made much use of Midrashic thinking. We must now pause briefly to consider its nature.

Five characteristics will suffice for the present purpose:

(i) Midrashic thinking reflects upon the root experiences of Judaism, and is not confined to their immediate—e.g., liturgical—reenactment.

(ii) For this reason Midrashic, like philosophical, reflection becomes aware of the contradictions in the root experiences of Judaism.

(iii) Unlike philosophical reflection, however, it a priori refuses to destroy these experiences, even as it stands outside and reflects upon them. For it remains inside even as it steps outside them, stubbornly committed to their truth. In the above-discussed two Midrashim, Rabbi Eliezer and Rabbi Yohanan both *reflect*, respectively, *upon* the events at the Red Sea and Sinai and remain immediately *at* the Red Sea and *before* Sinai.

(iv) Midrashic thought, therefore, cannot resolve the contradictions in the root experiences of Judaism but only express them. This expression (a) is fully conscious of the contradictions expressed; (b) is fully deliberate in leaving them unresolved; (c) for both reasons combined, is consciously fragmentary; and (d) is insistent that this fragmentariness is both ultimate for human thought and yet destined to an ultimate resolution. *Midrashic thought, therefore, is both fragmentary and whole.*

(v) Seeking adequate literary form, the Midrashic content can find it only in story, parable, and metaphor. Were they projected into the modern world, Rabbi Eliezer and Rabbi Yohanan might follow our present example and engage in a second-order philosophical reflection designed to explore the ontological and epistemological status of their Midrashim. However, this would not replace their first-order reflection which would remain committed to the truth of the root experiences of the Red Sea and Sinai even as it reflected upon them. Unless we shall find cause to judge otherwise,[23] to this day their stance remains normative for the Jewish theologian. Having engaged in a second-order reflection upon Midrash as a whole, he must himself retell the old Midrash—or create a new.[24]

## The Logic of Midrashic Stubbornness

We shall illustrate the above abstract contentions by a few concrete examples and confine these to the events at the Red Sea and Sinai.

We begin with a verse in the Biblical song sung at the Red Sea: "YHVH is a man of war, YHVH is His name" (Exod. 15:3). Why, the first of the two Midrashim we shall cite asks, are the seemingly superfluous words "YHVH is His name" added? Lest the idolatrous nations have an excuse for believing in many gods. For at the Red Sea He "appeared . . . as a mighty hero doing battle . . . at Sinai He appeared as an old man full of mercy." The words "YHVH is His name" are added, then, to teach that, while a God manifest in history manifests Himself differently according to the exigencies of the historical moment, He is, nevertheless, manifest in each moment as the one sole Power of every moment. "It is He who was in the past and He who will be in the future. It is He who is in this world and He who will be in the world to come. . . ."[25]

But our second Midrash shows that this universal revelation at the Red Sea would be wholly pointless if, in the case of the idolatrous nations, it fell on wholly deaf ears. However, it did not fall on deaf ears. All the nations joined in the words

"Who is like unto Thee, O Lord, among the gods" (Exod. 15:11)?

> As soon as the nations of the world saw that Pharaoh
> and his hosts perished in the Red Sea and that the king-
> dom of the Egyptians came to an end, and that judg-
> ments were executed upon their idols, they all renounced
> their idols, and opened their mouths and, confessing God,
> said: "Who is like unto Thee, O Lord, among the gods?"
> You also find that in the future likewise the nations of
> the world will renounce their idols.[26]

The universality of the sole Power manifest in a unique saving
event demands a correspondingly universal human *recognition*
of its universality, thus inspiring the poetic truth of the universal abolition of idolatry. We have cited two Midrashim: they
must be taken together.

But if taken together they reveal a contradiction. This
appears even in the first Midrash taken by itself: a God who,
by Himself, was, is, and shall be, yet must be present *differently* if His presence is to be *within* history. A contradiction
is more evident in the second Midrash taken by itself: the
nations forsake idolatry only poetically, and even then only
for a moment, a fact which makes a Messianic reference necessary. The contradiction is altogether inescapable when the two
Midrashim are taken together. The God who is Lord of history
was, is, and shall be sovereign as sole Power. Yet, even in a
supreme (albeit pre-Messianic) manifestation of His power,
He stands in need of human glorification; and the fact that
this glorification is momentarily given by all the nations reveals more poignantly the paradox of a subsequent relapse into
idolatry by the nations, Israel herself included. Confronting
this contradiction and commenting upon the verse "I will
glorify Him" (Exod. 15:7), Rabbi Yishmael asks: "Is it possible for a man of flesh and blood to add to the glory of His
Creator?"[27]

Rabbi Yishmael's question is radical. If the event of divine
saving Presence is complete without glorifying human recognition, then man, his abiding astonishment included, has lost

all significance for the Divine; and the Divine is sole Power, either because It is indifferent to history or because It overwhelms history. And if human glorification is required, then even a saving divine Presence—not to speak of a commanding Presence—is incomplete without it. No wonder Rabbi Shim'on Bar Yoḥai seeks to avoid the dilemma when he comments on the same Biblical verse as follows: "When I praise God, He is lovely; and when I do not praise Him, He is, so to speak, lovely in Himself."[28]

Rabbi Shim'on's answer does not, however, escape from the dilemma. How can human praise add to the divine glory and yet human failure to give praise not diminish it? Other rabbis (and Shim'on Bar Yoḥai himself in a different context) admit that human failure to give praise, so to speak, weakens the Power on high.[29]

Rabbi Yishmael himself answers his own question as follows: " 'I will glorify Him' means: I shall be beautiful before Him in obeying the commandments."[30] This answer, however, only serves to reproduce the dilemma in a still more ultimate form. A saving divine Presence may require only human recognition; a commanding divine Presence requires human action. The saving Presence may conceivably (if only momentarily) overwhelm human freedom. The commanding Presence cannot do likewise without becoming an intrinsic impossibility. Hence, as the Midrashic writers turn from the first to the second, they are forced to face up to an unmitigated paradox: " 'Ye are My witnesses, saith the Lord, and I am God' (Isa. 43:12). That is, when ye are My witnesses, I am God, and when ye are not My witnesses, I am, as it were, not God."[31] "When the Israelites do God's will, they add to the power of God on high. When the Israelites do not do God's will, they, as it were, weaken the great power of God."[32]

Taking all the cited Midrashim together, we find that the contradictions between divine transcendence and divine involvement and between divine Power and human freedom are not resolved but only expressed; and, indeed, that the expression could not be more frank, open, and conscious.

However, the Midrash holds fast to the *truth* of these contradictory affirmations even as it expresses their contradictoriness. In rabbinic theology, the term "as it were" *(k'b'yakhol)* is a fully developed technical term, signifying, on the one hand, that the affirmation in question is not literally true but only a human way of speaking; and, on the other hand, that it is a truth nonetheless which cannot be humanly transcended. The rabbinic thinker both *reflects upon* his relation to God and yet *stands directly before* Him, and his theology is consciously and stubbornly fragmentary.

But this does not exhaust the stubbornness of rabbinic thought. Conceivably one might speculate that the contradictions between divine transcendence and divine involvement and between divine Power and human freedom, all too real from the standpoint of man, are nevertheless transcended from the standpoint of God. And such speculation might (as, for example, in Kant)[33] take the form of a mere experiment of thought, or (as notably in Hegel)[34] that of a bold, actual ascent of thought to Divinity. In either case speculation might entertain the idea that history in the sight of God is other than history in human experience. For man, history is shot through with sin and suffering, only rarely lit up by the divine Presence; for God, it is transparent in the light of divine Power, and all darkness consists of insubstantial shadows. What is grimly real for human experience is, in the ultimate perspective, a cosmic game.[35]

Rabbinic thought stubbornly rejects a God playing such games and stubbornly holds fast to the reality of human history—even in the sight of God. To do otherwise would be, in the final analysis, to be unfaithful to the root experiences of Judaism—to a God present *in* history. How could Divinity be actually present as commanding unless obedience and disobedience made a real, ultimate difference? How could even a saving Divinity be actually present if the human perception of salvation were a matter of irrelevance?

All problems and dilemmas might resolve themselves if the saving divine Presence transfigured history. The divine saving Presence at the Red Sea, however, occurs in history and does not end or transfigure it. A much-quoted Midrash relates that when the ministering angels beheld the destruction of the Egyptians at the Red Sea they wanted to break out into song. God, however, reproved them, saying, "My children lie drowned in the Red Sea, and you would sing?"[36] This Midrash is much-quoted, for it encourages moralistic sermons concerning a God endowed with universal benevolence. The real content of the Midrash, however, is otherwise. *Even in the supreme but pre-Messianic moment of His saving presence God cannot save Israelites without killing Egyptians.* Thus the infinite joy of the moment—a moment in which even the maidservants saw what no prophet saw—is mingled with sorrow, and the sorrow is infinite because the joy is infinite. Thus the root experience in Judaism is fragmentary and points to a future consummation because of its fragmentariness. Thus God and man in Judaism pay each their price for the stubbornness with which they hold fast to actual—not "spiritual"—history.

## The Divine Presence and Catastrophe

But one may hold fast to history and yet do so not very seriously. Seriousness is tested in self-exposure to crisis situations. Rabbinic faith and thought were uniquely tested when, in 70 C.E., the Temple was destroyed by Titus, and still more so when, after the Bar Kochba revolt, Hadrian transformed Jerusalem into a pagan city (135 C.E.). Rarely in all the subsequent centuries was there to be a comparable clash between the root experiences of Judaism and present historical realities, and the well-nigh inescapable temptation of the times was to flee from history into either gnostic individualism or apocalyptic otherworldliness. The rabbis, however, remained *within* the Midrashic framework, and indeed, responded to the radical crisis with the most profound thought ever produced within that framework. This was because they both faced the present with unyielding realism and held fast to the root experiences of Judaism with unyielding stubbornness.[37]

Never before had the conflict between past and present been so radical. It is true that the God of past history, revealed as the God of all history at the Red Sea and Sinai, could often seem to be in conflict with present history. But one obvious response to this apparent conflict had always been to view suffering as deserved punishment, and in the earlier books of the Bible—notably Judges—this response had seemed totally adequate. To be sure, this was no longer so in the later books of the Bible. But the Book of Job questions this response only on behalf of the individual; and while the prophet Jeremiah protests against the prosperity of the wicked (Jer. 12:1) he is also able to view the destruction of the first Temple as a divinely willed punishment and the tyrant Nebukadnezzar as the rod of God's anger and His instrument (Jer. 25:9, 27:6, 43:10).

No rabbi described Titus as God's instrument. No rabbi understood the paganization of Jerusalem as an event which was divinely willed. To quote N. N. Glatzer, the rabbis

> could still understand a destroyed Jerusalem in terms of a divine plan for history, not, however, a pagan Jerusalem. Only because of despair of the realization of the kingdom of God on earth did the protest against Rome in the form of an armed national insurrection come to include the Tannaitic rabbis, who had hitherto not required that form, guided as they had been by the idea of a divine plan. Only thus can one understand the fact that Rabbi Akiba, who had hitherto shown great . . . patience vis-à-vis Rome, was now gripped by the national impatience and agreed with Bar Kochba. . . .[38]

It is true that in their catastrophic present the rabbis did not fail to explore and deepen already familiar lines of response. Thus the second destruction of the Temple, like the first, was viewed as a case of deserved punishment; and the punishment then, as before, became bearable because repentance would end the exile even as sin had caused it. And yet, the vast Roman

Empire was absurdly out of proportion to the sins of a handful of Jews; and to the repentance of that handful, ludicrously world-historical consequences had to be ascribed. Taken by itself and made absolute, then, this response was totally inadequate; it was bound to produce the view that God had destroyed His sanctuary without adequate cause, and that He was now distant and uncaring. "The concept of sin was insufficient to explain the course of events."[39]

Another long familiar response, too, if taken by itself and made absolute, was bound to lead to despair. In catastrophe the Psalmist had lamented that there was now a hiding of the divine Face and yet could hope that God's presence would again be manifest. The rabbis too spoke of a divine self-concealment. But was this enough? And was there any imminent hope? Not the second as far as one could anticipate. Not the first if the brute present realities were the evidence. According to Rabbi Shim'on Ben Gamliel, to write of the sufferings of the time was beyond all human power.[40] Rabbi Akiba, more full of hope than any other rabbi after the Temple had been destroyed,[41] was cruelly put to death by the tyrant Rufus after the Bar Kochba revolt. Was this how God "judged the righteous through the wicked"?[42] No wonder Rabbi Eleazar lamented that, ever since the destruction of the Temple, the gates of prayer were closed, and only those of tears were still open.[43] In earlier Jewish experiences the divine self-concealment had only been partial and temporary. Now it seemed otherwise. Now Rabbi Eleazar was forced to say: "Since the day of the destruction of the Temple, a wall of iron separates Israel from her Father in heaven."[44]

Had the rabbis staked all on the response of a divine self-concealment they would have lost the divine Presence in history in the time of Hadrian. Neither the past saving Presence nor the past commanding Presence could have continued to be reenacted. The past saving Presence would have been overwhelmed by the present catastrophe. Even the past commanding Presence would have vanished; there would have remained only obedience to commandments performed in God's absence.

This being the case, what hope for a Messianic divine Presence could have remained in an age of so total a divine self-concealment?

In this extreme crisis the rabbis struck out boldly in a new direction. Far from being unconcerned or concealed, God, so to speak, cried out every night in bitter lament, as with a lion's voice.[45] Rather than judge the righteous through the wicked, He, as it were, lamented His own decision; in causing His Temple to be destroyed and His people to be exiled, either He could not act otherwise or had grievously erred.[46] Here as elsewhere Rabbi Akiba is bolder than any other rabbinic theologian:

> Were it not expressly written in Scripture, it would be impossible to say it. Israel said to God, "Thou hast redeemed Thyself," as though one could conceive such a thing. Likewise, you find that whithersoever Israel was exiled, the Shekhinah, as it were, went into exile with them. When they went into exile to Egypt, the Shekhinah went into exile with them, as it is said, "I exiled Myself unto the house of thy fathers when they were in Egypt" (I Sam. 2:27). When they were exiled to Babylon, the Shekhinah went into exile with them, as it is said, "For your sake I ordered Myself to go to Babylon" (Isa. 43:14). When they were exiled to Elam, the Shekhinah went into exile with them, as it is said, "I will set My throne in Elam" (Jer. 49:38). When they were exiled to Edom, the Shekhinah went into exile with them, as it is said, "Who is this that cometh from Edom . . ." (Isa. 63:1). And when they return in the future, the Shekhinah, as it were, will return with them, as it is said: "That then the Lord thy God will return with thy captivity" (Deut. 30:3). Note that it does not say, "The Lord will bring back" (veheshib), but it says, "He will return" (ve-shab).[47]

What an altogether breath-taking turn of thought! The thought is breath-taking, for it is as if Rabbi Akiba had looked ahead to an exile unequalled in length and depth of misery and then taken the only turn of thought which could have saved Jewish faith during that millennial trial. The Jew would be in exile, but not cut off from the divine Presence. He could still hold fast to history, for the God who had been present in history once was present in it still and would in the end bring total redemption. Thus for nearly two millennia the Jew—mocked, slandered, persecuted, homeless—held fast to the God of history with a faith which, if not in principle unshakeable,[48] remained in fact unshaken.

But Rabbi Akiba's turn of thought raises one all-important question. A God in exile still commands, for He continues to be present. His presence still comforts, for it holds out hope for a future salvation as His past saving acts are remembered. But where, we must ask, is the "sole Power" or the "Creator of the world"?

As if in reply to this question, Rabbi Joshua ben Levi taught a century after Rabbi Akiba:

> The men of the Great Assembly are given this title because they restored God's crown to its former state. For Moses had said, "the great, powerful and awe-inspiring God." Then came Jeremiah and said, "The Gentiles are destroying His Temple: where then is the fear of Him?" Hence he omitted[49] the adjective "awe-inspiring." Then came Daniel and said, "The Gentiles are enslaving His children: where then is His power?" Hence he omitted[50] the adjective "powerful." Then, however, came the men of the Great Assembly and said: "On the contrary, this is His power, that He controls His anger and is long-suffering to evil-doers; and this is His fear—how could one nation exist among the nations of the world without the fear of the Holy One, blessed be He?"
>
> Why did these sages alter what Moses had ordained? Rabbi Eleazar replied: "They knew of the Holy One, blessed be He, that He is truthful, and would say nothing untrue about Him."[51]

We conclude, then, that the rabbis remained true to the catastrophic historical present, even as they remained faithful to the saving and commanding past. They remained stubborn witnesses to the nations that all history both stands in need of redemption and is destined to receive it.

## *Spurious and Genuine Contemporary Criticism*

This must suffice as an account of God's presence in history, as it is affirmed in Jewish tradition. At the outset we noted that this faith is the object of criticism, but also raised doubt as whether it falls prey to easy and obvious criticisms.

The account now concluded has confirmed these initial doubts. Thus, on one side, philosophical reflection soon discovers contradictions between divine Power and human freedom and between divine Providence over history and the evil which is within it; and, finding these contradictions insoluble, is apt to disconnect God with history speedily and without further thought. Such speed, we have now seen, is ill-advised. It would in any case be strange if Judaism and Christianity (both of which stand or fall with God's presence in history) had failed to note these contradictions in their long careers. We have found reasons for insisting that far deeper philosophical criticisms are necessary if they are to strike the mark.[52]

What is true of much general philosophical criticism offered on one side is also true of much specifically Jewish theological criticism offered on the other side. At the present time we are told, at one extreme, that Auschwitz is punishment for Jewish sins, and this is slander of more than a million innocent children in an abortive defense of God.[53] At the opposite extreme, we are told that precisely because this slander is inadmissible the God of history is impossible: a God concerned with Auschwitz must have decreed Auschwitz, and such a God is dead.[54]

We need not go beyond the ancient rabbis to reject both these theological doctrines. When the tyrant Rufus martyred Rabbi Akiba the rabbis did not slander either Akiba or his saintly contemporaries. And when Hadrian made Jerusalem a pagan city they, as it were, made God weep over it.

But it would be theological smugness of the gravest kind to dismiss all contemporary philosophical and theological criticisms along with these spurious ones. The ancient rabbis remained within the Midrashic framework; ever since the rise of the modern world, Jewish theological thought has confronted the challenge of secularism—that of stepping outside that framework and of calling it into question from outside. Moreover, ever since the Nazi holocaust, Jewish theology has faced the necessity of questioning the Midrashic framework from inside as well. The rabbis confronted Titus and Hadrian; they were spared the necessity of confronting Hitler. In the present age in which Jewish existence is uniquely embattled, the Jewish faith in God's presence in history is no less uniquely embattled. The Jewish theologian would be ill-advised were he, in an attempt to protect the Jewish faith in the God of history, to ignore contemporary history. For the God of Israel cannot be God of either past or future unless He is still God of the present.

## NOTES

1. *Mekilta de-Rabbi Ishmael*, ed. J. Z. Lauterbach (Philadelphia: The Jewish Publication Society of America [1933], 1949), II, 24 ff. (Subsequently cited as Mek.)

2. In the history of modern philosophy, the turning point is Kant. Kant himself still makes use of the concept of an external Providence, although it is doubtful whether he means to take it literally. His first great disciple—J. G. Fichte—internalizes it radically and without remainder.

3. See, e.g., his "Idea for a Universal History from a Cosmopolitan Point of View," *Kant on History*, ed. L. W. Beck (Indianapolis and New York: Bobbs-Merrill, 1963), pp. 11 ff.

4. *Summa Theologica* I qu. 22 art. 2: "A lion would cease to live if there were no slaying of animals; and there would be no patience of martyrs if there were no tyrannical persecution."

5. See below, pp. 70 and 73. This theme is more fully developed in my *Quest for Past and Future: Essays in Jewish Theology*

(Bloomington: Indiana University Press, 1968), ch. 1. This chapter was prepublished in somewhat different form in *Commentary* (August, 1968) under the title "Jewish Faith and the Holocaust."

6. Martin Buber, *At the Turning* (New York: Farrar, Strauss and Young, 1952), p. 61.

7. *Mek*, II, 30 ff.

8. See below, chapter III, pp. 93 ff.

9. On this point, see further my *Quest for Past and Future*, pp. 3 ff., 112 ff., 249 ff.

10. For this concept I am indebted to Irving Greenberg's concept of "orienting-experience" (see above, Preface). I here prefer the term "root experience" because I wish to analyze the intrinsic characteristics of the experience before considering its historical efficacy. It would be desirable to find a word uniting both connotations, but I have not been able to find such a word.

11. See below, pp. 13 ff.

12. *Mek*, I, 135 ff. The passage refers to the commemoration of the Exodus as a whole.

13. In the Passover Haggadah we find the following statement:

> It was not one only who rose against us to annihilate us, but in every generation there are those who rise against us to annihilate us. But the Holy One, blessed be He, saves us from their hand.

It is only a small exaggeration for me to say that whether, and if so how, the contemporary religious Jew can still include this sentence in the Passover Seder liturgy is the paramount question behind my entire investigation in this book.

14. Martin Buber, *Moses* (New York: Harper Torchbooks, 1958 [London: East and West Library]), pp. 75–77. (Italics added.)

15. See *Mek*, I, 216:

> Rabbi Eliezer says, The Holy One, blessed be He, said to Moses: "Moses, My children are in distress. The sea forms a bar and the enemy pursues. Yet you stand and say long prayers! Why do you cry unto Me?" Rabbi Eliezer was wont to say, there is a time to be brief in prayer, and a time to be lengthy.

16. *Mek*, I, 237.

17. *Midrash Rabbah*, Song of Songs, V 16 § 3, trans. Maurice Simon (London: Soncino Press, 1961), pp. 252 ff.

18. *Mek*, II, 212.

19. On this subject, see further my *Quest for Past and Future*, ch. 14.

20. See, e.g., *Midrash Tanḥumah*, Yitro.

21. On this point, see Buber's treatment of "moment gods," *Between Man and Man* (Boston: Beacon Press, 1955), p. 15.

22. *Bab. Talmud*, Tractate Berakhoth 33b. Rabbi Hanina, the author of this statement, adds that "God has in His storehouse nothing but the fear of heaven."

23. See below, chapter II.
24. See below, chapter III.
25. *Mek*, II, 31 ff.
26. *Mek*, II, 59 ff.
27. *Mek*, II, 25.
28. *Sifre Deut.*, Berakhah § 346.
29. *Ibid.*; *Sifre Deut.*, Ha'azinu § 319.
30. *Mek*, II, 25.
31. *Midrash Rabbah*, Psalms, on Ps. 123:1.
32. *Midrash Rabbah*, Lamentations, on Lam. 1:6.
33. See his *Critique of Judgment*, § 76.
34. See my *The Religious Dimension in Hegel's Thought* (Bloomington: Indiana University Press, 1968), especially chs. 5 and 6.
35. Hegel rejects and possibly is able to avoid this conclusion. But if he can avoid it it is because his rise in thought to Divinity is a Christian or post-Christian possibility.
36. *Bab. Talmud*, Tractate Megillah 10b.
37. This is comprehensively expounded and documented by N. N. Glatzer, *Untersuchungen zur Geschichtslehre der Tannaiten* (Berlin: Schocken, 1933). The present section of this chapter is greatly indebted to Glatzer's masterful work.
38. *Ibid.*, p. 5.
39. *Ibid.*, p. 106.
40. *Bab. Talmud*, Tractate Shabbath 13b.
41. Once four rabbis—Gamliel, Eleazar Ben Azaryah, Joshua, and Akiba—walked by the ruins of the Temple. Suddenly they saw a fox emerging from the place which had once been the Holy of Holies. The others wept. Akiba, however, laughed, for he saw this event as confirming a prophecy of doom and was thus strengthened in his faith in another prophecy which promised redemption (*Midrash Rabbah*, Lamentations, III:18).
42. *Midrash Rabbah*, Lamentations, III:17.
43. *Bab. Talmud*, Tractate Berakhoth 32b.
44. *Ibid.*
45. *Bab. Talmud*, Tractate Berakhoth 3a.
46. *Ibid.*
47. *Mek*, I, 114 ff. See Lauterbach's notes which make it clear that the Scriptural proof-texts must be given a special interpretation in order to bear out Rabbi Akiba's Midrash.
48. See below, chapters II and III.
49. In Jer. 32: 16 ff.
50. In Dan. ch. 9.
51. *Bab. Talmud*, Tractate Yoma 69b.
52. For my treatment of some of these, see chapter II.

53. Z. M. Schachter writes:

> In response to Nazi hostilities, we judged all Germans to be inhuman, predatory beasts, and the Germans returned the compliment. They were the stronger, and we, by definition, the vermin to be exterminated. In short, *the Holocaust was partially caused by Jews who did not think it worthwhile, or even possible, to reprove the Germans.* (*The Religious Situation, 1968,* D. R. Cutler, ed. [Boston: Beacon Press, 1968], p. 81.)

The only excuse for Schachter's statement is a desperate desire to exonerate God. (i) It is false that Jews (Schachter himself included) judged all Germans to be beasts; the fatal Jewish error, if any, was the opposite—an inability to believe, until it was too late, that Jews were destined for wholesale murder. (ii) It is absurd to believe that any Jewish "reproving" of Nazis might have had a beneficial effect; the exact opposite would have occurred. Schachter is not alone among the religiously minded to fall prey to this error. Martin Niemoeller is reported to have said recently that he sinned in failing to attempt to convert Hitler. Perhaps the attempt was his Christian duty. But can he seriously believe that he might have succeeded?

54. See R. L. Rubenstein, *After Auschwitz* (Indianapolis and New York: Bobbs-Merrill, 1966); also "Homeland and Holocaust: Issues in the Jewish Religious Situation," *The Religious Situation, 1698,* pp. 39–64, 102–11. For my own fragmentary attempts to cope with the Holocaust, see below, chapter III, as well as the article referred to in note 5, and "Jewish Values in the Post-Holocaust Future: A Symposium," *Judaism* (Summer, 1967), pp. 266–99.

# II    The Challenge
of Modern Secularity

## *The God-Hypothesis*

In an oft-told story the eighteenth-century astronomer Laplace outlines his astronomical theory to Napoleon; and the emperor, less interested in astronomy than in theology, complains that he misses God in it. Laplace proudly replies: "Sire, I do not require that hypothesis."

The story has often been told, presumably because it has a modern lesson. Yet exactly what makes the lesson modern is far from obvious. Thus, for example, the rejection of unnecessary assumptions goes back to the Middle Ages: Maimonides disposes of superfluous miracles, and Ockham's famous "razor" states that entities should not be multiplied beyond necessity. Maimonides, however, retains some miracles,[1] and Ockham does not reject God.

The Laplace story does reject God. Even so it is not clear that it is either very modern or very radical. Laplace subscribes to a mechanistic materialism in terms of which everything, if not actually explained, is at least in principle explainable. Is this why Laplace can dispense with the God-hypothesis? Would he be prepared to retain it if he were forced to take a more modest view of science—if all things were neither explained nor explainable but rather if mystery deepened as knowledge advanced? If so, his iconoclasm would not be very radical after all. Nor would it be very modern. For we have long rejected the kind of scientism of which Laplace is a representative; we do take a more modest view of the scope of science.[2] We have not, however, returned to the God-hypothesis. We should all consider a scientist to be, as it were, switching gears if, having talked about mathematical formulae and empirical experiments, he suddenly talked about God. Laplace may not have had the right reasons for his conclusion. The conclusion itself is certainly unexceptionable: in modern scientific discourse the God-hypothesis is not required.

What, then is the right reason for Laplace's conclusion? Not that modern science knows more than pre-modern science (although certainly it does), but rather that it has a radically different methodological principle. Pre-modern science (which is not clearly distinct from metaphysics) does not hesitate to infer absolute and transcendent causes from relative and empirical effects. Modern science (which is emancipated from metaphysics) rejects this inference as in principle illegitimate, and is supported in this by all significant modern philosophy. The followers of Immanuel Kant give their support. So do the followers of Auguste Comte. And, on this particular issue, nearly all contemporary philosophers are either Kantians or Comteans.

Contemporary science and philosophy thus rule out the God-hypothesis not only when scientific explanations are at hand but also when they are not at hand, and this despite the fact that mechanistic materialism has long been rejected. We know what to look for in a scientific explanation—and it is not God. Indeed, inasmuch as the hypotheses looked for are empirically verifiable, and God is not, the God-hypothesis is something worse than an unnecessary intruder. Strictly speaking it is a contradiction in terms. Here at last we have a reasonably up-to-date version of Laplace's answer to Napoleon. And few would doubt that the answer is right.

But did Napoleon ask the right question? There is in current theology much loose talk about the "death" of the "God-hypothesis";[3] yet one may well ask whether this talk has any application either to the God of the philosophers or to the God of Abraham, Isaac, and Jacob.

Of the two, the God of the philosophers is the more likely candidate. Thus, when in Aristotle's Physics God appears as the prime mover of nature, He seems suspiciously close to the God-hypothesis.[4] Yet when this same God appears in His own right in the Metaphysics,[5] He clearly transcends these quasi- or pseudo-scientific contexts. As for Plato, his case is more obvious: he bids all seekers after the Divine to "leave the starry heavens alone."[6] The God of pre-modern metaphysics (which remains bound up with pre-modern science) is thus not obviously identifiable with or reducible to the God-hypothesis.

The case becomes less obvious still as we turn from pre-modern to modern metaphysics. If modern science is emancipated from metaphysics, then, by the same token, modern metaphysics is emancipated from modern science. This emancipation is complete in Kant, Hegel, and Heidegger—to list at random modern metaphysicians with very different commitments. Not one of these thinkers comes anywhere close to accepting a God-hypothesis; even so, in very different ways, they all find the God of the philosophers inescapable. Is this God, then—now or ever—an explanation, or, if so, is He reducible to His explanatory function?

Modern positivism gives an affirmative answer. Ever since Auguste Comte, it asserts that metaphysics is pre-scientific explanation and that it vanishes when genuine or scientific explanation comes upon the scene. Yet it never demonstrates but only asserts this doctrine. It nowhere shows signs of an effort to understand the God of the philosophers; and, in reducing Him to the God-hypothesis, it presupposes what it claims to prove.

Positivistic criticism is still more dubious when it is brought
to bear upon the God of Abraham, Isaac, and Jacob. For Comte
and his followers, religion, like metaphysics, is a precursor of
science. The one is pre-scientific "rational" explanation; the
other is pre-scientific "mythological" explanation: and both
vanish without a legitimate trace when science proper comes
upon the scene. They vanish, we say, *without a legitimate trace.*
Pre-modern skepticism disposes of philosophical and religious
answers; modern positivism disposes of the questions as well.
For, in the first place, modern science does not find the
"Absolutes" looked for in philosophical and religious explanation. In the second place, it does not continue to look for
these, for it seeks "relative" and not "absolute" explanations.
Hence, in the third place, if religion and philosophy are primitive science, all "Absolutes" were a mere logical mistake all
along.

But *is* religious myth primitive science and reducible to
an explanation? The gods are evidently pre-scientific, but even
they are not evidently explanations, and this is dramatized by
the fact that when they are "demythologized" this is done—
among other forces—by the Biblical God.[7] This God, moreover, is no explanation, even if the gods are. What to the
Bible are idolatrous myths may be explanations of sorts, but
this is just what makes them idolatrous; and in destroying
these explanations the Biblical myths put no rival explanations
in their place.

Thus the Biblical creation myth does not explain cosmic
origins. The Greek cosmogonies may do so, for they derive
the present world of man from a prior world of gods. The
Biblical creation account, however, reveals the incommensu-
rability of an infinite God with all things finite. Hence it
does not and cannot explain the origin of the world but only
assert it: "Creation" is *the* primordial miracle. And just as
Genesis fails to explain cosmic origins so the Book of Job
fails to explain evil; it ascribes to Job's friends, not to Job himself, the pursuit of such idolatries. Positivistic doctrine asks
us to believe that the Biblical God is a God-hypothesis. But

what, one must ask, is a God-hypothesis which does not explain?[8]

It explains, it may be rejoined, inexplicability itself. This neo-positivistic view may be summed up as follows. Biblical faith originates as a myth which takes good fortune to be sufficient proof of righteousness, and ill fortune to be sufficient proof of sin. So crude an explanation, however, in due course breaks down under the impact of experience, and Biblical faith then continues to survive by means of refuge in the unknowable. There is the revealed and the explained; but there is also the concealed and the inexplicable. Good fortune is proof of God's mercy and love; ill fortune merely proves that His ways are not our ways. For Biblical faith, in short, it is "heads-I-win-and-tails-you-lose"; its God has acquired the logical peculiarity that empirical evidence may confirm Him but that it is systematically unable to falsify Him. But, so the positivist concludes, this implies not that the Biblical God has ceased to be a hypothesis but merely that He has become an improper one: the logical peculiarity referred to, far from saving the God-hypothesis, is only an additional ground for its rejection.

This line of thought, unlike much other positivistic thought, is held to be philosophically respectable to this day.[9] Yet it owes much of its plausibility to the uncritical identification of two sets of categories. We have found the categories "revealed" and "concealed" to be essential to Biblical and rabbinic thought. But are these automatically or obviously identifiable with the categories "explained" and "inexplicable"? The examples of rabbinic thought given in the previous chapter are enough to arouse extreme skepticism. To the rabbis not even moments of supreme darkness in history are *simply* inexplicable while, at the same time, not even moments of supreme light are moments in which all is explained. Thus, in times of catastrophe there may be protest, and this confronts inexplicability but will not accept it. There may also be revelation without explanation, for the exile of a God who is sole Power is inexplicable.[10] Again, there are times of salvation which yield no explanation. Thus the great event at the Red Sea—an event which causes even the maidservants to see what no prophet saw—creates an abiding wonder; and no explanation can show why a God who is sole Power cannot save Israelites without killing Egyptians.[11] Indeed, one wonders whether for the rabbis even the Messianic future, which will reveal all, will explain all. Will it explain the death of even a single child?

Doubtless the rabbis struggle to explain the events of history. But, to put it cautiously, one must doubt whether "explanation" and "inexplicability"—categories which come naturally and hence uncritically to the modern, scientifically oriented mind—are central to their thinking. As for the corresponding term "God-hypothesis," we may cast all caution to the winds and deny its applicability categorically. The God-hypothesis is an *inferred* and hence *necessarily absent* God. The God of the prophets and rabbis, however, is a God capable of *presence.* Having created heaven and earth, He, as it were, *Himself* walks in the garden. Having tested Job's faith, He confronts him with His inscrutable power; inscrutability is not a mere inference from the course of events. The God of Israel, in short, is a present God. He and the God-hypothesis have nothing in common.

But then, this conclusion might have been guessed all along. Consider these facts of Jewish history. The Jewish people originated in the root experiences of a saving and commanding divine Presence. It continued to reenact these root experiences through the millennia, holding fast, even in grim catastrophe, to a God who, having saved once, was saving still and whose commandments had not lost their living presence. It carried the Torah through every exile and remained faithful to the covenant through every turn of fortune. Such was the power of a God present in history, or—if we wish to suspend all commitment—of Jewish faith in such a divine Presence.

What, in contrast, might have been the power of a God-hypothesis merely inferred from the facts of history? First, this hypothesis would have been only probable even in the best of times. Second, it would have rested on the general course of human history of which Jewish history was but a small segment. Third, this small segment itself was for the most part as full of inexplicable pain and suffering as any segment of history anywhere. The view that such a hypothesis could ever have been framed—or, if framed, been preserved—or, if preserved, have caused the Jewish people and their faith to survive through four millennia—defies all belief.

## *The Divine Presence and Subjectivist Reductionism*

Did Napoleon, then, ask a completely wrong question? And did Laplace give a wholly irrelevant answer? By no means. We have thus far dismissed insignificant challenges of modern, scientifically inspired secularism to the Jewish faith. Its significant challenge we have yet to face.

This emerges only as we turn Laplace's criticism away from the stars and the universe, toward and against the Biblical and rabbinic faith in the divine Presence itself. Consider these obvious secularist reactions to all the major religious affirmations described in our first chapter. The maidservants at the Red Sea did not "see"; they merely *thought* they saw. The Israelites at Mount Sinai did not "hear"; they merely *imagined* they heard. No such thing as a "sole Power" was ever present, making "transparent" the current nexus of cause and effect; there was at most only a *feeling* of such a presence and of such a transparency. And while those gripped by this feeling may have been overwhelmed by "abiding astonishment"— by a wonder only "deepened" by causal explanations—these conditions do not hold true of the modern critic when he reflects upon these facts. For that critic is filled not with abiding astonishment but only with scientific or historical curiosity;

and the curiosity ceases to abide when the facts are explained.

Here at last we have come upon the central secularist assault upon Biblical and rabbinic faith. This latter affirms an *immediate* divine Presence. In the view of the secularist critic, however, what is immediate is at most the *feeling* or *appearance* of such a presence, and any *actual* divine Presence is an *inference* to account for this feeling or appearance. To be sure, the believer is not aware of making such an inference; but then, there are unconscious as well as conscious inferences. In short —so the secularist concludes—the God of Biblical and rabbinic faith remains a hypothesis after all; only it is not framed to account for the earth or the stars or three-story universes, but rather for religious experience. And, as need hardly be added, this God-hypothesis is no more needed or wanted than any other. Here at long last we have reached the point at which Napoleon's question, properly brought up-to-date, meets with Laplace's answer, properly redirected. And the result is a modern challenge to faith for which there is no pre-modern precedent.

No pre-modern precedent exists because faith in the pre-modern world could seek refuge, when challenged, in authoritarianism. The divine Presence could then be asserted on the authority of Scripture without. It could be asserted also on the authority of experience within—an experience which, essentially private, was infallible for belief and inaccessible to the criticism of unbelief. However, the modern believer cannot accept the divine Presence on the authority of Scripture; he can at most accept any authority of Scripture because of a divine Presence manifest in it.[12] Moreover, as regards private, authoritative experiences, no Jewish believer could ever stake much on these. Ezekiel's vision may have been an experience of this kind. What happened at the Red Sea and Sinai, in contrast, were public events, accessible even to the maidservants to the extent to which they were accessible at all.

These public experiences are therefore not immune to modern, scientifically inspired, secularist criticism. Consider a modern secularist miraculously projected into the past so as to share the experience of the Israelite maidservants. He would observe the natural-historical event at the Red Sea (assuming that there was such an event to be observed). He would see what the maidservants saw—nothing less than the presence of God. Indeed, while the experience lasted, he would partake, like the maidservants, of an abiding astonishment. Unlike the maidservants, however, he would cease to abide in this state of astonishment once immediacy had yielded to critical, scientifically inspired reflection. For reflection would reconstruct the whole course of events. There had appeared to be a miraculous event; the event, however, had only *appeared* to be miraculous, and this appearance called for an explanation. There had seemed to be a divine Presence; Divinity, however, had only *seemed* to be present; and the feeling that this had been so stood in need of explanation as well. And whatever the terms in which such an explanation might be sought, an *actual* divine Presence would not be among them. The actual divine Presence in history, as asserted by millennia of Jewish (and Christian) faith, has vanished.

A radical conflict has thus manifested itself between Biblical and rabbinic faith, on the one hand, and modern, scientifically inspired secularism on the other—a conflict for which the pre-modern world has no precedent. From our first chapter it has emerged that the Jewish faith, originating in root experiences of a saving and commanding divine Presence, remains in a state of *immediate openness* to such a Presence as throughout history it reenacts the ancient root experiences— open to the possibility of a divine Presence even in times when the actuality is only a memory and a hope. We have now come upon a stance of *critical reflection* which dissipates every supposed divine Presence into mere feeling and appearance. This critical reflection does not ignore the evidence of faith; it rather hands it over for explanation, and the terms in which the explanation is given or promised are such that what we have referred to as the Midrashic framework lies in ruins.

## The Mutual Irrefutability
## of Faith and Secularism

But it is one thing to admit the incompatibility of faith and modern secularism, quite another to admit that faith is refuted by such a secularism. We have elsewhere termed the secularism presently under consideration subjectivist reductionism, and argued that Jewish faith and modern secularism are mutually irrefutable.[13] Here we shall not reproduce but only summarize the argument. For Bertrand Russell (who articulates secularism) existence is shut off from the divine Presence, for there is only a feeling of presence and nothing more. For Martin Buber (who articulates Jewish faith) existence is open to the presence of God, and feeling is a mere by-product. The first articulates a faith, for he presupposes and does not prove that God is a mere inference—one rightly discarded. The second too articulates a faith, for he is open to the possibility of a divine Presence even if that Presence is not actual. Russell places reflection above immediacy, making it its interpreter and judge; thus its dissipation is preordained. Buber places immediacy above reflection, for this latter, cut off from the divine Presence, is left with the mere feeling which is its by-product; thus is preordained the impotence of reflection to dissipate the divine Presence.

The two positions are obviously irreconcilable. Less obvious, but no less important, is that they are mutually irrefutable as well. Believing immediacy cannot refute secularist reflection, for this divides the evidence of faith into "objective" natural-historical events and "subjective" feelings of divine Presence, and the divine Presence is not among either class of "data," or legitimately inferred from them. Subjectivist reductionism is irrefutable by faith.

The reverse is equally true. The "sole Power" is present in and through a natural-historical event for an "abiding" wonder.[14] Secularist criticism—historical, sociological, psychological—does not refute this immediate Presence when it splits up religious immediacy into "objective" physical "data" and "subjective" psychological ones. This split already presupposes subjectivist reductionism.

The secularist, therefore, cannot refute but only convert the religious believer. This possibility, too, is mutual. We have above projected the modern, scientifically inspired secularist among the maidservants at the Red Sea, and observed him persist in his secularism. One possibility, however, was then not considered. Conceivably the secularist might partake of an astonishment radical enough to sweep aside all mere curiosity, to overwhelm all destructive reflection, and to assume a permanent quality which could only be deepened by causal explanations. Were this to occur, the secularist would have turned away from his secularism: he would have turned to, and have been turned by, the presence of God.

## The Self-Exposure of Faith to Modern Secularism

If modern secularism cannot refute but only contradict Jewish faith, why has it been, and continues to be, a challenge which is without precedent? When Titus destroyed the second Temple, and Hadrian paganized Jerusalem, the rabbis adhered stubbornly to the root experiences of Judaism. No such stubbornness has been shown by their descendants after the Emancipation cast them into the modern world and exposed them to modern secularism. The difference, moreover, has not been in quantity or degree alone. The ancient rabbis remained within the Midrashic framework. Modern Jews have stepped outside that framework and called it into question. This is obviously true of Jews abandoning their Jewish heritage. But it is true also of those who, in one form or another, are concerned to preserve it. Except for more or less marginal groups, they believe in the necessity of coming to terms with modern secularism.

This fact is easily confirmed. Whereas pre-modern history produced one normative Jewish religious response, modern history has inspired a variety of Jewish responses, vying with each other in their claims, if not to normativeness, then to modernity. To stay with a previous example, the pre-modern Passover Seder was the celebration of the divine saving Presence at the Red Sea, a celebration which implied—whatever the changing fortunes of contemporary history—that the Divinity which had saved once was saving still and would ultimately bring total salvation. The modern Passover Seder is different things to different Jews. At one extreme it is a celebration of human freedom and nothing more. In the middle there is lurking doubt as to whether what is celebrated is the presence of God or the human discovery of the idea of God. Even at the other extreme there is doubt, if not concerning the validity of the Midrashic framework, then at any rate concerning its present relevance; in the modern secular world, can the presence of God be more than a mere memory?

What is this need, almost universally felt, for self-exposure to modern secularism, by a faith which secularism cannot refute? On this as on many other questions, it is fruitful for Judaism to establish contact with Christianity. The Christian like the Jewish faith is irreconcilable with secularism. It too is irrefutable by modern secularism. Yet recent Christian theology feels a significant need for self-exposure to the modern secular world, and this despite the risk of surrender to secularism. What inspires this necessity? *The fact that, in modern times, the secular world is "where the action is," and that a God of history must be where the action is.* Yet self-exposure to secularity involves self-exposure to secularism—the critical dissipation of the very possibility of the presence of God.[15]

Jewish no more than Christian faith can avoid this self-exposure. For a Christian to do so would be to seek flight into a worldless church. For a Jew it would mean flight into the pre-modern Ghetto. But if God is a God of history He must be a God of contemporary secular history also. Either flight is impossible.

## *Faith as Immediacy*
## *After Reflection*

It has thus emerged that faith and modern secularism do not, after all, confront each other on even terms, their mutual irrefutability notwithstanding. By the terms of its own self-understanding, modern secularism can afford to ignore faith, and, if the presence of God were to shatter it, this would cause radical surprise. By the terms of *its* self-understanding, however, modern faith (Jewish or Christian) cannot afford to ignore secularism. Religious immediacy must expose itself to the threat of subjectivist-reductionist reflection, and modern Jewish faith can authentically preserve the Midrashic framework only after having stepped outside that framework, thus calling it into question. Such a stance of faith was called by Søren Kierkegaard "immediacy after reflection."

Let us illustrate this stance of faith in a manner relevant to our overall purpose. Consider the case of an imaginary but not altogether atypical modern Jew who has celebrated the Passover Seder in a spirit of religious immediacy ever since his early childhood. His has been no empty performance but rather a participation in the Exodus of his ancestors, affirming that the saving God of the Exodus saves still and will ultimately bring final redemption. But as boyhood gives way to adolescence, and modernity makes its presence felt, critical reflection injects itself into religious immediacy; and in due course the discovery occurs that, whatever the historical "data" referred to in the Passover story, the presence of God is not among them; and that, whatever the terms in which modern historical or psychological reflection may seek to explain these data, the God-hypothesis is neither necessary nor permissible. Along with these discoveries there arises doubt, or even despair, as to the possibility and meaning of any present celebration of the Passover. Our imaginary young Jew, in short, has become critical of his earlier religious immediacy.[16] He has not yet become critical, however, of his present criticism.

We shall let him reach that third and final stage with the help of a passage which, quoted in full earlier in this book, has had a crucial influence on our entire discourse. The passage is from Martin Buber's *Moses*, and its presently relevant part is the following:

> The real miracle means that in the astonishing experience of the event the current system of cause and effect becomes, as it were, transparent, and permits a glimpse into the sphere in which the sole power, not restricted by any other, is at work.[17]

We have previously discussed what the passage describes. We must now turn to the nature, scope, and limitations of the description. Buber writes from a historical point of view.[18] As a historian, he can do no more than describe, for to identify himself with the standpoint described would be to abandon the historian's proper role and adopt a religious commitment. At the same time, he may, as a historian, do no less than describe. Conceivably he might, instead of describing the astonishing experience of the ancient believers, explain it in terms of some modern system of cause and effect, and to do so may even seem to be required by critical objectivity. However, such explanations (at least if, unlike those given at the standpoint of immediacy *itself*, they dissipate the wonder) explain away in the process of explanation; they represent, not historical impartiality, but rather a commitment to secularism. Genuine impartiality requires the historian to suspend judgment between faith and secularism. And this insight produces what we have called the *third* and *final* stage at which our hypothetical young Jew attains to criticism of criticism.

More precisely, this is one aspect of that final stage. The other consists of the recognition on the part of our imaginary Jew that, whereas as a historian he may and must suspend judgment, he cannot do likewise as a man and Jew, if only because every Passover Seder constitutes a challenge to participation. How can he participate? *No longer* in a religious immediacy which has never thought of stepping outside the Midrashic framework. *Not at all* in a stance of critical reflection which stands outside only and merely looks on.[19] Nothing is possible except an immediacy after reflection which is and remains self-exposed to the possibility of a total dissipation of every divine Presence, and yet confronts this possibility with a forever reenacted risk of commitment.

This stance of faith is part of what Buber referred to when he spoke of an "eclipse of God."[20] The metaphor is inspired by the Biblical "hiding" of the divine Face. At the same time, it also points to a uniquely modern condition. Pre-modern Jewish faith did not step outside the Midrashic framework even in times of catastrophe; hence it could hold fast even then, without radical doubt, to the memory of and hope for a divine Presence. Modern Jewish faith has stepped outside the Midrashic framework, suffering a loss of innocence which remains even in times when the divine Presence is an unquestioned or unquestionable reality. Self-exposed to a secularism which would dissipate every claim to a divine Presence into mere feeling or appearance, it comes face to face with the possibility that man is in principle cut off from God. Hence it is only by virtue of an unprecedented stubbornness that the modern Jewish believer can be a witness, in and to the modern secular world, of God's presence in history. Such is the testimony of a faith which is immediacy after reflection.

## On the "Death" of God

But there is yet a second form of modern secularism which, while less universal than the first, poses a far deeper challenge. The secularism thus far dealt with in this discourse *dissipates* God's presence in history. The secularism commanding our attention from now on *transforms* that presence. The first destroys a mere hypothesis which is far removed from the God of Judaism; the second pronounces the death of God Himself— a God far too close for comfort to the God of Biblical tradition. The first secularism rejects the history of faith as a simple falsehood, and hence bids Jews become "normal";[20a] the second regards past faith as a past truth now become anachronistic, and demands of Jews a creative self-transfiguration.

We have used the expression "death of God." This goes back to Friedrich Nietzsche, but has lately come into wide popular usage, a fact calling for a preliminary distinction between serious and merely sensationalist employments. The difficulty or even impossibility of modern religious belief would constitute the death, not of God, but at most of belief in Him; and the falsehood of all religious belief would indicate not that God is dead but rather that He was never alive. To be sure, the expression "death of God" is in any case metaphorical. But there is metaphorical, as well as literal, truth and falsehood.[21]

The metaphor, first, can be true only if God, now somehow dead, was once somehow alive. Second, this event can concern Jewish or Christian faith only if it is historical rather than natural: gods dying (and rising) in nature have long been demythologized by these religions. Third, to concern Jewish (as distinct from Christian) faith, the event must be universal and cannot be part of the history of Christendom only. All talk of the "death" of God sounds in any case far stranger to Jewish than to Christian ears, and the Jewish reader of Nietzsche cannot miss the Christian overtones.[22] When he adds that the term "death of God" has a long history—for Nietzschean atheism is preceded by Hegel's speculative trinitarianism, and Hegel in turn alludes to Luther—a Jew may well wonder whether the "death" of God is a Jewish issue even when it is a serious one. Perhaps it is serious for a faith for which God has become finite and incarnate in history. But is it serious for a faith whose God throughout history remains "He who was in the past and He who will be in the future . . . , He who is in this world and He who will be in the world to come"?[23]

But, on the one hand, the God of Israel, while beyond history and infinite, is also present in history to man in his finitude. And, on the other hand, the Nietzschean death of God is not a limited and contingent event which is without permanent or universal effect. In this event God dies *away into* man, leaving man both forever Godless and endowed with a wholly new freedom. The event is, therefore, world-historical and—so Nietzsche holds—it divides *all* history into before and after.

Perhaps this is why Nietzsche utters his prophecy through the mouth of a madman.[24] The death of ancient pagan deities never produced madness but only expectation of new gods. After the Nietzschean death of God, however, there is no waiting for new gods. All possible gods have died. And, since they have died away into man, the birth of a new man is required— a man endowed with new, superhuman, as yet inconceivable powers. Nietzsche's madman *is* mad, then, because he comes both too late and too soon: too late to have a god for company;[25] too soon to be able to bear the new solitude.[26]

Because of these world-historical claims, the Nietzschean death of God challenges Jewish as well as Christian faith. Moreover, its challenge is profound and radical. For, unlike the secularism discussed hitherto, this secularism constitutes a *religious* challenge. Subjectivist reductionism destroys the God-hypothesis; Nietzsche's atheism overcomes God Himself. The God-hypothesis is a finite projection, always false and the product of mere ignorance, superstition or neurosis; the God of Nietzsche is an *infinite* projection, true while it lasted, and producing a world-historical transformation when the old truth turns into an anachronism.[27] In both forms of secularism the otherness of the Divine is denied. But while in the first case this otherness was never authentic, in the second it was authentic while it lasted; and while in the one case the denial leaves no result, in the other, denial is at once affirmation. For to deny the otherness of the Divine is to affirm the potential divinity of the human. Subjectivist reductionism, in short, is a destruction of religion which has no real power over the religiously minded. Nietzsche's atheism is a new rival religion, the passion and power of which match the old.

Even so, Jewish faith would not face up to this new religion if it viewed Nietzsche as its sole prophet. The claims of such a religion would in any case be suspect if it had only one great prophet. Moreover, in Nietzsche this religion has features—aristocratic aestheticism and return to Hellenism, to name but two—which are too alien to basic Jewish commitments to produce a serious confrontation. It is quite otherwise, however, with what, for want of a more accurate term, may be called left-wing Hegelianism—a tradition which begins with Ludwig Feuerbach, culminates in Karl Marx, and gives in the great contemporary Ernst Bloch impressive proof of its continued vitality. Here, as in Nietzsche, there is a dialectical denial of the otherness of the Divine which produces the affirmation of a new, human (or more-than-human) freedom. But unlike in Nietzsche the new freedom is here embodied, not in great aristocratic individuals, but rather in new forms of human community; and for this reason—again unlike in Nietzsche[28]—history as a whole assumes a forward, Messianic direction. Nietzsche recalls the Greeks. Left-wing Hegelianism (though it is rarely aware of this fact) recalls the Jews, and for this reason it challenges Jews far more intimately and radically. It is precisely because it shares the Jewish Messianic expectation that this post-religious religion negates Jewish religious existence absolutely, as it denies the God of Israel and affirms a universal man raised above his Jewish, religious, human limitations.

## Jewish Existence and Secularized Messianism

Jewish Messianism always requires the particularity of Jewish existence. Its God is universal; but, because His presence is in history and does not (or not yet) transfigure history, it can only be a particularized presence, and for this if for no other reason, it is a fragmentary presence. The saving divine Presence at the Red Sea had revealed its fragmentariness, if only because the Egyptians were drowning; the divine commanding Presence at Mount Sinai had been fragmentary, if only because it could be rejected as well as accepted; the law was not yet put in the inward parts (Jer. 31:33). For the Jew to experience or reenact such a fragmentary divine Presence is, on the one hand, to be *singled out* by it and, on the other, to be made to *hope for wholeness*; that is, to be made a witness to the Messianic future and to remain stubbornly at this post until all has been accomplished. This Jewish particularity, however, has been a scandal, first, to ancient pagans (who denied that history stood in need of redemption) and, subsequently, to Christians (to the degree to which they hold that the redemption affirmed by the Jewish testimony has already arrived).

Jewish particularity remains a scandal to modern secularism. *Mutatis mutandis*, subjectivist reductionism resembles ancient paganism when, denying the Divine, it calls—in one form or another—for Jewish "normalization," secularized Messianism resembles Christianity inasmuch as both claim to transcend Jewish Messianism and consequently view Jewish particularity as an anachronism. Of the two forms of secularism the second (being a rival faith) poses the far more profound threat to Jewish survival. Few Jewish converts to Christianity ever rivalled in passion and effectiveness those Jewish Marxists who, in their own eyes become universal men, preached a universal Jewish duty to dissolve into humanity in general. Nor is this surprising. The Messianic faith has been implicit in Judaism since its origins. Such has been its passion and impatience that Jews again and again accepted Messianic claims, only to be subsequently disappointed. If, nevertheless, for nearly two thousand years they have resisted the Christian Good News even at the price of continued exile, it has been because acceptance seemed a betrayal of the Jewish post so long as this world was unredeemed. Is it any wonder that, when a secular, this-worldly redemption was at last being proclaimed, Jews accepted it with a unique passion, and that they sought to contribute to the new humanity by means of Jewish self-dissolution into it? Of such Jews, the historian J. L. Talmon writes as follows:

> Their fatherland was the Revolution which had no frontiers; their country was mankind or the proletariat. . . . What other people had even remotely experienced universalist Messianism with the same intensity? . . . One of Rosa Luxemburg's letters from prison to a Jewish friend [says]: "Why do you pester me with your Jewish sorrow? There is no room in my heart for the Jewish troubles." And she goes on to speak most eloquently of the Chinese coolies and of the Bantus in South Africa. Twenty-five years later, after the Germans had occupied it, there was not a single Jew left alive in Rosa's native Zamosc. . . .[29]

We ask: what is queer about a faith which produces Jewish compassion for the suffering of Bantus but only impatience with, or even contempt for, that of fellow Jews? Nothing is queer, it may be replied, and it is certainly true that one such as Rosa Luxemburg may not be judged by hindsight. Not knowing the facts referred to in Talmon's shocking last sentence, she could sincerely view the genuine Jewish destiny to be, in the Age of Revolution, self-dissolution in mankind.

Yet for the contemporary critic the question remains. Admittedly the old Jewish Left cannot be judged by hindsight-knowledge. The new Jewish Left, however, itself possesses this knowledge. Why are there today so many humanity-minded Jews on the Left who protest against war in Vietnam but refuse to protest against antisemitism in Russia and Poland? Or, who will defend all anticolonial wars for liberty but condemn Israel's war for life itself? In the Russia of today, every nationality (the former German enemy included) has the right to cultural self-expression; Jews alone are denied that right. In the eastern Europe of today there must surely be countless memorials to the various peoples victimized by Nazism; there is no memorial, however, for the Jewish victims at Babi Yar, and the memorial at Auschwitz is to victims-of-fascism-in-general. What perversity can give a faith in humanity two totally different connotations—for every other people on earth, the right to life; for the Jewish people, the duty of spiritual if not physical suicide? And what vastly greater perversity can make Jews themselves accept such a faith?

## *Anti-Judaism in Left-Wing Hegelianism*

It may be replied that there is no perversity in the minds of the new Left, non-Jewish or Jewish. As sincere as the old, it may believe that the old Jewish Left was not wrong but merely betrayed; that while Trotsky's universalism was once betrayed by Stalin's nationalistic, antisemitic particularism, this will not happen again.

But before arriving at so comforting and comfortable a conclusion the new Jewish Left would be well advised to wonder whether, if betrayal there once was, it does not antedate Stalin by nearly a century. Nineteenth-century left-wing Hegelian thought denied all the false old gods; and, since the denial was dialectical, it produced new human truths from the old religious falsehoods. But while the old gods were all false some were more false than others. Still more important—indeed, crucially—while all the other religions had a degree of truth, Judaism alone was declared to be simply undialectically false. Only a single major nineteenth-century left-wing Hegelian—Moses Hess—did any kind of justice to the old Jewish God in the process of denying Him, and he was led to Zionism. In the view of both the first and the greatest of the nineteenth-century left-wing Hegelians—respectively, Ludwig Feuerbach and Karl Marx—Judaism was not now dead but rather had never been alive. No wonder the dialectical destruction of such a religion resulted, not in the liberation of the Jewish people, but rather in the demand for Jewish group-suicide.

We shall dwell briefly on Feuerbach and Marx. For Feuerbach Jewish "particularism" is sheer "egoism." Indeed, egoism is "the principle of Judaism." The Jew worships himself rather than the one universal God, and, projecting such self-worship on the universe, he makes it absolute. Hence while even idolatrous polytheism has a degree of religious truth, Jewish monotheism is simply, undialectically false. The Greeks "looked abroad into the wide world that they might extend their sphere of vision; Jews to this day pray with their faces toward Jerusalem." To this day "their God is egoism" and—which is worse—"egoism in the form of religion."[30] No mention is ever made by Feuerbach of the countless Jewish martyrs to the One God, of the centuries of patient Jewish waiting and working, of the hope that all men would be redeemed. We thus conclude that Feuerbach, the atheist, has rejected the Christian God; but that this one-time Christian theologian has not rejected Christian antisemitism. His image of Judaism is nothing but slander.

From Feuerbach we turn to Marx. Marx may or may not share Feuerbach's antisemitism. He does, in any case, repeat his slander. Indeed, just as his philosophy is more radical than Feuerbach's, so is his slander of Judaism. Unlike Feuerbach, Marx refuses to "seek the secret of the Jew in his religion." Instead, he will seek "the secret of religion in the real Jew." What does he find? "The profane basis of Judaism . . . [is] practical need, self-interest. What is the worldly cult of the Jew? Huckstering. What is his worldly god? Money."[31] No wonder Marxists of less orthodox persuasion find this awkward, and seek ways to mitigate blame. This, to be sure, is understandable, but it is not always forgivable. Erich Fromm writes that Marx "said some harsh (and in my opinion not always correct) words about what he thought was the Jewish religion."[32] This formulation is a piece of apologetic dishonesty for which there is no excuse.

But the question is not praise or blame but rather truth or falsehood and, in the case of a dialectical thinker such as Marx, whether gross falsehood in one point of doctrine can fail to have fatal consequences in others. In Marx's view, Judaism is a sheer, undialectical falsehood; and the capitalism with which it is bound up is a form of life which one day will vanish without a trace. Is it any wonder that he held that Jews too would vanish without a trace once socialism had arrived? Other peoples would and should survive, be liberated, and form part of the human family. In the case of Jews, mere insistence on group survival would be enough to constitute hostility to mankind. Only if they committed group-suicide and ceased to be Jews, could they be liberated and join the human family. Such are the horrendous dialectical consequences which may be drawn, and all too often were in fact drawn, from Marx's slander of the Jewish religion. And, in view of the enormous influence of Marx's thought for well over a century, it is not far fetched to connect this nineteenth-century slander either with twentieth-century Soviet antisemitism, or with the compulsive anti-Zionism which today bedevils even the noncommunist Left.[32a]

## *Ernst Bloch*

How might a more genuine and more truthful encounter with Jewish religious existence affect the left-wing Hegelian dialectic? We need not rely on speculation, for we find in Ernst Bloch a great contemporary example. Not the least part of the greatness of this great thinker lies in the well-nigh inexhaustible sympathy which he brings to the vast varieties of the past even as he criticizes and transcends them. This sympathy, in his case, extends to Judaism, and—virtually unheard of in Western philosophy—to rabbinic as well as to Biblical Judaism.

What kind of Judaism emerges from Bloch's sympathetic understanding? For Feuerbach and Marx, the Jewish God is a law-giving tyrant who rules over slaves. For Bloch, He is the herald of freedom, and Jews are His first, prophetic witnesses. For Feuerbach and Marx the God of Judaism is a jealous particularist. For Bloch, He strains towards universality. For Feuerbach and Marx, He never ceases to be a reactionary. For Bloch, He is a revolutionary ever since the Exodus from Egypt. In short, whereas Feuerbach's and Marx's Judaism is "egoism," Bloch's Judaism is Messianism, and there can be no doubt that, whatever the limitations of Bloch's understanding, he is far closer to the truth.

Moreover, Bloch's Judaism is close to his own, post-religious truth—so close that only a single dialectical turn is necessary in order to attain it. The religious Jew keeps praying for the Messianic future even as he works for it, and he remains dependent on a divine promise and commandment. Still required is a revolutionary turn which makes an end of all prayer and obedience, denies divine otherness, and produces the new future freedom. There remains in Judaism an unresolved conflict between divine otherness which inhibits man, and the Messianic hope which promises liberation. This conflict will disappear in a post-religious, post-Jewish, atheistic Messianism in which Judaism is at once fulfilled and superseded. For Feuerbach and Marx, the Jewish God was never alive. For Bloch, He dies only on the threshold of the promised land.

It is thus not surprising that for Bloch, unlike for Feuerbach and Marx, the Jewish people survive the death of their God. They survive Him in Palestine, for if the "preservation" of other "small peoples" is "gratifying" or even "necessary" from a "national . . . point of view," so is that of the Jewish people. They survive Him in the Diaspora, for the "best Jews" will preserve their "ancient relationship with all that is meant by the words 'end of . . . Babylon' and 'new world.'" Why then is Bloch nevertheless certain that Judaism dissolves into a "Jewish component" of a universal reality and that the particular Jewish people can have post-religious significance only if they transcend their particularity? He writes:

> In our age, the age of the Soviet Union and of the movement toward Soviet Unions [Moses Hess] . . . would no longer locate his intended Jerusalem in the physical Jerusalem. An end of the tunnel is in sight, certainly not from

Palestine, but rather from Moscow;—*ubi Lenin, ibi Jerusalem.*[33]

With these words, written during the Second World War but explicitly endorsed as late as 1959 (when Soviet antisemitism was obvious to all except those unwilling to notice it), Bloch's Messianism, and indeed left-wing secularist Messianism as a whole, shows itself to be a modern form of a very old Jewish phenomenon, namely, premature Messianism. This is an honorable phenomenon, for it is born of love for the poor and oppressed, and of impatient waiting. Its modern form is more honorable than most, for it seeks an unequivocally this-worldly salvation and is more bound up with all nations and races than any pre-modern form ever had a chance to be. Even so, in the age of Hitler and Stalin, it is clear that this Messiah, like so many who have preceded him, is false.

## Death of God and Eclipse of God

But the new premature Messianism also differs from all the old forms. Its difference is the dialectical move by which God dies away into "free" universal humanity, and Jews, once singled-out witnesses, die away into that humanity. The secularist makes this move; a religious Jew must ask why such a move, never previously made, should be considered a modern necessity. Not because the divine Presence is not demonstrable, for the new faith is as undemonstrable as the old. Not because the old faith has become a minority faith, for neither the new nor the old faith makes its case on the basis of majorities. *The dialectical move is considered necessary because only if the God other-than-man is dead can human freedom be real.* From Feuerbach to Bloch and Sartre this is the ever-recurring theme, and from a recent Christian God-is-dead theologian we hear:

God . . . is the transcendent enemy of the fullness and the passion of man's life in the world, and only through

God's death can humanity be liberated from that repression which is the real ruler of history.[34]

Beyond all doubt the God here under attack is the God of Israel, or, more precisely, His commanding presence. Yet He is not that God but only His caricature. We have seen long ago that the rabbis were not unaware of the threat of a divine commanding Presence. Indeed, they experienced a far more radical threat than Marx or Nietzsche ever dreamt of, for it was not to freedom but to existence itself: the descent of the first commandment at Sinai produces not partial frustration but absolute terror. But it was precisely in the midst of this terror that the rabbis experienced, in abiding astonishment, a Grace which was in the commandments, and which made a free response to a divine commanding Presence a human possibility. As experienced and taught in Judaism, the divine commanding Presence does not repress human freedom but exalts it; and a Jew singled out by that Presence does not groan under the burden of the law but rather rejoices in the commandments.[35]

As a believing Jew today testifies to this possibility he bears witness against the proclamation of the death of the old God. He would in any case cast doubt on the proclamation of the new freedom. When Nietzsche and Marx issued their respective clarion calls they could be believed. Today they sound unbelievable to all except belated theological celebrants of the modern secular world. It is ironical that these celebrations should coincide with the widespread renunciation, on the part of realistic secularists, of their former Messianic expectations. And it is not accidental that the God-is-dead theologies, proclaimed as epoch-making only a few years ago, are already dead themselves.

In any case, no Jew in the age of Auschwitz—and of persisting antisemitism despite and because of Auschwitz—is likely to place Messianic expectations in the modern secular world. It follows by no means, however, that Auschwitz, and all the other tragedies and despairs of our age, by themselves warrant a "return to religion." For, as will be shown in the following chapter, secularist and believer inhabit the same world, and there is in this age hope and despair both within faith and without it. It was not in behalf of an easy religious optimism that Buber dismissed the phrase of the "death of God" as a "sensational and incompetent saying,"[36] and himself affirmed an eclipse of God. To be sure, there is hope with this image, for an eclipse may come to an end. Yet in what is perhaps the last statement he wrote on this subject, Buber ends on a note of stark realism:

> These last years in a great searching and questioning, seized ever anew by the shudder of the now, I have arrived no further than that I now distinguish a revelation through the hiding of the face, a speaking through the silence. The eclipse of God can be seen with one's eyes, it will be seen. He, however, who today knows nothing other to say than, "See there, it grows lighter!" he leads into error.[37]

## NOTES

1. See, e.g., *Guide for the Perplexed*, II, chs. 25, 29, 35. Among the miracles retained are the salvation at the Red Sea and the revelation at Sinai.

2. Ernst Mach writes:

> The French Encyclopedists of the eighteenth century imagined they were not far from a final explanation of the world by physical and mechanical principles; Laplace even conceived a mind competent to foretell the progress of nature for all eternity, if but the masses and velocities were given. (Quoted by W. C. Dampier, *A History of Science* [New York: Macmillan, 1946], p. 213.)

Dampier adds: "Few would venture to make such a sweeping statement nowadays, and definite indications have quite recently appeared to suggest that such determinism is impossible."

3. Dietrich Bonhoeffer indulged in some loose talk when he wrote:

> there is no longer any need for God as a working hypothesis, whether in morals, politics or science. Nor is there any need for such a God in religion or philosophy (Feuerbach). (*Letters and Papers from Prison* [London: SCM Press], p. 163.)

Whether "God in religion or philosophy" ever was a "working

hypothesis" is a question here simply begged, a fact underlined by the invoking of the authority of Feuerbach.

Anglo-Saxon followers of Bonhoeffer have been much more crass than Bonhoeffer himself, who is careful to distinguish the "present" God from the God-hypothesis. Thus John A. T. Robinson's influential *Honest to God* (London: SCM Press, 1963) simply assumes that Biblical spatial imagery (God "up" or "out" there) rests on an outdated "three-storey-universe," and that it has no legitimate symbolic significance when it is detached from such a universe. (Careful pondering, e.g., of Ps. 139 might have been enough to call both assumptions into question.) Again, such a work as Paul van Buren's *The Secular Meaning of the Gospel* (New York: Macmillan, 1963) does not merely assume but argues that the Biblical God is an anachronistic God-hypothesis; but his argument depends heavily on a philosophical linguistic empiricism whose applicability to religious faith is itself highly questionable. See further my "Elijah and the Empiricists," *The Religious Situation 1969* (Boston: Beacon, 1969), pp. 841–68.

4. See *Physics*, Book VIII.

5. See *Metaphysics*, Book XII, especially chs. 7 and 9. For Aristotle it is physics which proves the existence of God whereas metaphysics contemplates His essence. Yet even the Aristotelian "physical" proof would be "metaphysical" by modern standards, inasmuch as it argues not only from the moved to the mover but also from potential to actual being. The mere fact of modern science does not, therefore, *ipso facto* outmode it.

6. Plato, *Republic*, 530.

7. In Hegel's view the Greek gods are demythologized, in different ways, by three historical forces, all antedating modern science: Greek philosophy, the Biblical God, and the Roman Empire which, in assembling all gods in the pantheon, relativizes and thus destroys them.

8. The reader may wonder why we devote space to classical positivism when philosophers have for the most part abandoned even logical positivism, its more subtle successor. The reason is that it still dominates the thinking on religious and philosophical matters of many social scientists and even theologians. See, for example, Harvey Cox, *The Secular City* (New York: Macmillan, 1965).

9. A single example must suffice. In a "University Discussion" on "Theology and Falsification," the participants (R. M. Hare, Basil Mitchell, and I. M. Crombie) all responded to the thesis (offered by Anthony Flew) that such a statement as "God loves us" is a hypothesis which can resist falsification only because it has died the "death of a thousand qualifications." While Hare questioned the God-hypothesis in principle even he did not consider the possibility

of God's presence in history and its implications. (*New Essays in Philosophical Theology,* Anthony Flew and Alasdair MacIntyre, eds. [London: SCM Press, 1955], pp. 96–130.) As of this date the *New Essays* have had five impressions, and the "University Discussion" has been discussed and anthologized in widely used introductory texts. On this subject, see more fully my essay referred to in note 3.

10. See above, p. 28.

11. See above, p. 25.

12. See my "The Dilemma of Liberal Judaism," *Quest for Past and Future* (Bloomington: Indiana University Press, 1968), pp. 130–47.

13. "On the Eclipse of God," *Quest for Past and Future,* pp. 229–43.

14. See above, pp. 12 ff., where we have been careful to stress that the three terms introduced by Buber—the present sole Power, the natural-historical event, and the abiding astonishment—are all needed, and are "intelligible only in their relation."

15. To corroborate this judgment—that it is the inescapability of the modern secular world as a whole and not, for example, modern science taken in isolation, which is the religious challenge—here we merely point to the fact that Bonhoeffer took care to distinguish between a God-hypothesis to be discarded and a divine Presence to be accepted, and yet created for his Anglo Saxon disciples, who sought Christian self-exposure to the modern-secular world, the spectre of the loss of the divine Presence in this act of self-exposure. See further my "On the Self-Exposure of Faith to the Modern-Secular World," *Quest for Past and Future,* pp. 278–305.

16. The terms in which we have described the stage of reflection (which makes the subject a detached observer of physical and psychical "data") are, deliberately, loose enough to include many forms. Our hypothetical young Jew may simply have acquired the general temper of criticism; or he may have become involved in specific critical inquiries among which might be not only psychology, sociology, or history but also modern Jewish scholarship.

17. *Moses,* p. 77. See above, pp. 12 ff.

18. He describes his concept of miracle as one which "is permissible from the historical approach." (*Op. cit.,* pp. 75, 77.)

19. Kierkegaard describes such a stance as one which is "infinite in reflection" because it pretends that it can ignore existence.

20. Buber, *Eclipse of God* (New York: Harper and Bros., 1952) is essentially concerned, not with the historical catastrophes of our age, but rather with "the assumption that the outcome of the crisis in which religion has entered depends essentially upon the judgments which are made by modern ontological or psychological thought" (p. 87). In a discussion with Buber in which this writer

was present, one participant confessed that while he was on occasion capable of prayer he found himself compelled at once to reflect upon his prayer, to reduce it to a mere subjective-psychic function, and thus to destroy it. Buber replied that this was the basic spiritual sickness of our age.

20a. For a discussion of this implication, see below, pp. 79 ff.

21. The Christian "God-is-dead" theology seems already itself to be dead. One reason for its quick demise would appear to be that its proponents never had more than the slogan in common; another, that even its sole radical and serious proponent (T. T. J. Altizer) found it impossible to show how Christianity could survive the death of God. (See my essay cited in note 15.) The "death" of God, if taken seriously, would seem to lead, not into a chimerical "religionless" Christianity (or Judaism), but rather into a post-religious humanism such as that of Nietzsche and Marx. This is not to deny that there might be other, as yet unexplored, post-religious possibilities.

22. In the famous passage in which the madman proclaims the death of God (The Gay Science, § 125), the divine death itself, the knives of his human murderers, the corpse of God, and the call for a requiem are all images which could not easily be given meaning in a Jewish context. It should be added that the Nietzschean imagery has pagan as well as Christian connotations, and that these are at times explicitly anti-Judaic, such as when he makes the gods laugh themselves to death when one of their number, "forgetting himself," becomes jealous and pronounces, "thou shalt have no other god before me." (The Portable Nietzsche, ed. Walter Kaufmann [New York: Viking, 1954], p. 294.)

23. See above, p. 21.

24. The Gay Science, § 125.

25. In a letter to Franz Overbeck, dated 2/7/1885, Nietzsche writes: "For all those who somehow had a 'god' for company, what I know as 'solitude' did not yet exist."

26. Nietzsche makes his madman say:

> I have come too soon; my time has not yet arrived. This momentous event is still on its way and wanders about; it has not yet reached the ears of men. Thunder and lightening need time, as does the light of the stars. Human actions require time even after they have been done, in order to be seen and heard. To men this deed is still farther than the farthest stars—and yet they have done it themselves. (The Gay Science, § 125.)

27. Nietzsche's madman says:

> We are all His murderers. But how could we do such a thing? How could we drink up the ocean? Who gave us a sponge wherewith to wipe off the whole horizon? What did we do when we cut the earth loose from the sun? Where does it move now? Where

> do we move? Away from all suns? Are we not falling . . . backwards, sideways, forwards, in all directions? Is there still any up and down? Are we not straying through infinite Nothingness? . . . How can we comfort ourselves, who are the murderers of all murderers? The Holiest and Mightiest that the world possessed hitherto has died under our knives: who will wipe the blood off us? . . . *(Ibid.)*

It is impossible to imagine any positivist (or, for that matter, most of the recent Christian God-is-dead theologians) writing in such a vein.

28. Nietzsche writes:

> it would be extraordinarily dangerous to believe that humanity as a whole would continue to grow while the individuals become flabby, equal, average. . . . Humanity is an abstraction." (Quoted by G. A. Morgan, *What Nietzsche Means* [New York: Harper Torchbooks, 1965], p. 200.)

29. "The Jewish Intellectual in Politics," *Midstream* (January, 1966), p. 10.

30. *The Essence of Christianity* (New York: Harper Torchbooks, 1957), pp. 112, 114, 115.

31. "The Jewish Question," *Early Writings*, trans. and ed. T. B. Bottomore (New York: McGraw-Hill, 1964), p. 34. The essay abounds in observations on subjects of which Marx demonstrably lacks even the slightest knowledge, such as the Talmud.

32. *Op. cit.*, preface, p. v. Fromm rightly attacks the cold war use made by Dagobert Runes in his edition of Marx's essay (*A World Without Jews* [New York: Philosophical Library, 1959]). But just as reprehensible is his own no less propagandistic unqualified denial that Marx was an antisemite. That it is simply false to assert that "Marx was a true internationalist who had no preference for any nation, and who was critical of all, never respecting the taboos of national feeling" (op. cit., pp. iv ff.), is carefully demonstrated by Edmund Silberner, "Was Marx an Anti-Semite?" (*Historia Judaica*, 1949, pp. 3–52.) Indeed, the evidence adduced by Silberner makes it virtually impossible to clear Marx of the charge of antisemitism.

Fromm is not alone among left-wing propagandists who deny every antisemitic stain in Marx's thought. But the *non sequitur* to end all *non sequiturs* must surely have been reached by Harry Pachter when he writes: "Marx, being descended from rabbis, could not be anti-semitic, of course. . . ." ("Jewish Righteousness and Antisemitism of the Left," *Salmagundi* [Spring 1968], p. 8.)

32a. The Arab socialist attitude toward Israel draws inspiration from Marx's essay, which exists in an Arabic translation. See, for example, Adib Dimitri, "The Jewish Question and Scientific Socialism," *Al-Katib* (Cairo, August, 1967).

33. *Das Prinzip Hoffnung* (Frankfurt: Suhrkamp, 1959), pp. 712,

713, 711. Bloch also writes that "the economic-social revolution disposes at once of the Jewish question" (p. 711), and the context leaves no doubt as to his view that this has already happened in the Soviet Union. It is important to mention, however, that in 1968 Bloch signed a document clearly at odds with his earlier views. A *Joint Declaration by Twenty Representatives of the German Left Concerning the Middle East* states, among other points, (i) that democratic socialists must look critically at bolshevism; (ii) that any hopes placed in the "third world" must not "degenerate into an oversimplified black-and-white portrayal . . . : the inclusion of Israel in a capitalist-imperialist front simply does violence to the facts"; (iii) that, after Nazism, the survival of the Jewish people can no longer be taken for granted: "If Jewry has any future to look forward to at all, it is thanks to Israel"; (iv) that "the deterioration of . . . [Israel's] relationship with the Eastern Bloc does not emanate from Israel"; and (v) that "the Left would lose its credibility for all time to come if, through one-sided sympathy for the Arabs, it were to contribute to a new Auschwitz." (*Jewish Frontier* [November, 1968], pp. 8, 10, 11.)

In view of the fact that Bloch, even in his earlier work, understood Jews as a living people, not as an ideological stereotype, one is not surprised at his ability to reach, albeit belatedly, the above conclusions. But, one wonders, how has this recognition affected his Messianic interpretation of the "progressive" parts of the contemporary world?

34. T. T. J. Altizer, *The Gospel of Christian Atheism* (Philadelphia: Westminster Press, 1966), p. 22.

35. See above, pp. 15 ff. On this subject, see further my "The Revealed Morality of Judaism and Modern Thought," and "On the Self-Exposure of Faith to the Modern-Secular World" (*Quest for Past and Future*, pp. 204–28, 278–305).

36. Buber, *Eclipse of God*, p. 91.

37. *The Philosophy of Martin Buber*, ed. P. A. Schilpp and Maurice Friedman (La Salle: Open Court, 1967), p. 716.

# III    The Commanding Voice of Auschwitz

## *The Madman's Prayer*

The writer Elie Wiesel tells the story of a small group of Jews who were gathered to pray in a little synagogue in Nazi-occupied Europe. As the service went on, suddenly a pious Jew who was slightly mad—for all pious Jews were by then slightly mad—burst in through the door. Silently he listened for a moment as the prayers ascended. Slowly he said: "Shh, Jews! Do not pray so loud! God will hear you. Then He will know that there are still some Jews left alive in Europe."

This tale calls to mind another tale referred to earlier in this discourse. Friedrich Nietzsche, too, tells a story of a madman bursting in on a group of men, uttering dreadful words about God. There, however, all similarity ends. For in the one tale there is horror because God is dead; in the other, because He is alive. One madman addresses God's murderers; the other, His victims. The first hopes that tomorrow some men will be free; the second fears that tomorrow all Jews will be dead. An abyss yawns between the prophecy of a dead God and a prayer addressed to a living God, but spoken softly lest it be heard.

Yet all these contrasts, however stark, pale in comparison to another. The Nietzschean event of the death of God may have its ambiguities. Thus it signifies the loss of old and also the gain of new treasures, and it inspires a mixture of mourning and celebration. In one crucial respect, however, it lacks all ambiguity; and this is true of Nietzsche's own version of the event, as well as of those of his present-day Christian followers. The death of God occurs in the inward realm of the spirit alone, and nowhere else. Such catastrophes as it includes are internal catastrophes only; and even the vast contemporary external catastrophes, such as Auschwitz and Hiroshima, appear only, as it were, by accident. In Wiesel's story, however, Auschwitz is not an accident. It is and remains the center of the event, and this despite and because of the fact that God is part of it. Wiesel's is a Jewish story, for it refuses to spiritualize history.[1] Nietzsche's is a Christian, pseudo-Christian, or post-Christian[2] story, for in it spiritualization of history is of the essence. And yet in the story in which Auschwitz is accidental God is dead, and in the story in which it is essential He is alive.

The two madmen, therefore, suffer two wholly different kinds of madness. As we have seen, Nietzsche's madman comes too late to have gods for company and too soon to be able to bear the new solitude;[3] his present madness is therefore of the spirit alone, and so are the two sanities—the old, past sanity, which was companionship with the gods, and the new, future one, which will be human solitude. In the sharpest possible contrast, Wiesel's madman has all along held fast to a God who is Lord of actual history, its external events included. His was a sanity which held fast to God and to the world and was unable to disconnect the two. Hence it now turns into an unheard-of madness. For if sanity is not of the spirit only, but rather contact with the world (and with God in and through the world), then such sanity, when the world is Auschwitz, is destroyed by madness. And if insanity consists of flight from the world (and to gods who have themselves fled from the world),[4] then such flight, when the world is the Nazi holocaust, is necessary if even a shred of sanity is to remain. Jewish prayer, however, cannot achieve this sanity, for it cannot disconnect God from the world. Hence any Jewish prayer at Auschwitz is madness. Such is the terrible tale, such is the terrible Midrash of Wiesel's madman.

## The Midrashic Framework and the Holocaust

This Midrash has no precedent in the ancient Midrash, for the Nazi holocaust has no precedent in ancient Jewish history—or medieval or modern. All history is full of unjust suffering; this term, when applied to Auschwitz, is hopelessly inadequate. Many past Jewish martyrs died for their faith; Hitler murdered Jews on account of their "race"[5]—believers and unbelievers alike. And if we can trace "racial" antisemitism as far back as medieval Spain (when converted as well as unconverted Jews were persecuted), we must also concede that "racial" antisemitism is one thing; the very thought of genocide, another. Nor did the Nazi genocide of European Jewry remain in the realm of mere thought. The Christian theologian, J. Coert Rylaarsdam, deliberately using hyperbole in order to shock Christian conscience, asserts that for Christians there have generally been only two "good Jews," a dead Jew and a Christian.[6] This suggests a connection between a Christian antisemitism which gives Jews a choice and a "racial" one which may lead to the thought of Jewish genocide.[7] Still, contemplation is not action. Long before Hitler the crime was contemplated.[8] Hitler executed it. And so carefully planned was the execution, so relentlessly and systematically was it pursued, that there is little doubt that, had he won the war, not a single Jewish man, woman and child would today be left alive on earth.

The Nazi genocide of the Jewish people has no precedent

within Jewish history. Nor, once the necessary distinctions are carefully made, will one find a precedent outside Jewish history. Today such distinctions are recklessly ignored. There is violent and indiscriminate talk of genocide, and an American college professor passes beyond the bounds of all decency when he compares the American campus to the Auschwitz murder camp.[9] Even actual cases of genocide, however, still differ from the Nazi holocaust in at least two respects. Whole peoples have been killed for "rational" (however horrifying) ends such as power, territory, wealth, and in any case supposed or actual self-interest. No such end was served by the Nazi murder of the Jewish people. Fantastic efforts were often made to hunt down even a single Jew; Adolf Eichmann would not stop the murder trains even when the war was as good as lost, and when less "sincere" Nazis thought of stopping them in an effort to appease the victorious Allies. The Nazi murder of Jews was an "ideological" project; it was annihilation for the sake of annihilation, murder for the sake of murder, evil for the sake of evil. Where would one find a counterpart, among any criminals, to Eichmann, who, with the third Reich in ruins and ashes, declared that he would jump laughing into his grave because he had sent millions of Jews to their death?[10]

Still more incontestably unique than the crime itself is the situation of the victims. The Albigensians died for their faith, believing unto death that God needs martyrs. Negro Christians have been murdered for their race, able to find comfort in a faith not at issue. The more than one million Jewish children murdered in the Nazi holocaust died neither because of their faith, nor despite their faith, nor for reasons unrelated to the Jewish faith. Since Nazi law defined a Jew as one having a Jewish grandparent, they were murdered because of the Jewish faith of their great-grandparents. Had these great-grandparents abandoned their Jewish faith, and failed to bring up Jewish children, then their fourth-generation descendants might have been among the Nazi criminals; they would not have been among their Jewish victims. *Like Abraham of old, European Jews some time in the mid-nineteenth cen-*

tury offered a human sacrifice, by the mere minimal commitment to the Jewish faith of bringing up Jewish children. But
unlike Abraham, they did not know what they were doing,
and there was no reprieve.[11]

The Hitler regime had a "research" institute on the "Jewish question,"[12] enlisting learned scholars in the task of thoroughly understanding Jews and Judaism in order to be able
thoroughly to destroy both. We ask: has it succeeded in one
part of its aim, though failing in the other? Hitler failed to
murder all Jews, for he lost the war. Has he succeeded in destroying the Jewish faith for us who have escaped?

We hardly dare ask so appalling a question. Yet it forces
itself upon us. Mid-nineteenth-century European Jews did not
know the effect of their action upon their remote descendents
when they remained faithful to Judaism and raised Jewish
children. What if they had known? Could they then have
remained faithful? Should they? And what of us who know,
when we consider the possibility of a second Auschwitz three
generations hence. (Which would we rather have our great
grandchildren be—victims, or bystanders and executioners?)
Yet for us to cease to be Jews (and to cease to bring up Jewish
children) would be to abandon our millennial post as witnesses
to the God of history.

In view of such terrifying questions which arise, it is
not strange that until a few years ago Jewish theological
thought has observed a nearly total silence on the subject of
the holocaust. A recent questionnaire does not even include
it among the questions, and few of the respondents refer to
it in their replies.[13] Is this nothing but cowardice? Such is the
view of a "radical" Jewish theologian, who asserts that "the
facts are in," that the traditional theological "options" are
clear-cut, obvious, and "will not magically increase with the
passing of time," and that the conclusion is certain: the Midrashic framework is shattered forever by Auschwitz; the God
of history is dead.[14]

But might it not be a well-justified fear and trembling,
and a crushing sense of the most awesome responsibility to

four thousand years of Jewish faith, which has kept Jewish theological thought, like Job, in a state of silence, and which makes us refuse to rush in where angels fear to tread, now that speech has become inevitable? The critic, who rightly states that it "remains emotionally impossible for most Jews to deal . . . with the trauma of Auschwitz," is quick to attribute the silence of others to a defence mechanism which makes them deny that Auschwitz ever happened.[15] What assures him of his own capacities to deal with the trauma—or stills his fear that some other mechanism may cause him to utter words which should never have been spoken? We need not go beyond his jarring expression "the facts are in." Will all the facts ever be in? And what, in this case, are the facts apart from the interpretation? The statistics? The novelist Manès Sperber, himself a survivor, writes:

> Even if all the firmament were made of parchment, all the trees were pens, all the seas ink, and even if all the inhabitants of the earth were scribes, and they wrote day and night—they would never succeed in describing the grandeur and the splendour of the Creator of the universe.
>
> Fifty years separate me from the child who learned to recite these opening lines of a long Aramaic poem that had been transmitted, with an unalterable oral commentary accompanying it, from generation to generation. I come back to the resonance of these phrases whenever I bring myself, once again, to the realization that we will never succeed in making the hurban—the Jewish catastrophe of our time—understood to those who will live after us. The innumerable documents that we owe to the indefatigable bureaucracy of the exterminators, the many narratives by witnesses who miraculously escaped, the diaries, chronicles and records—all these millions of words remind me that "even if all the firmament. . . ."[16]

Clearly the long theological silence was necessary. Silence would, perhaps, be best even now, were it not for the fact that among the people the flood-gates are broken, and that for this reason alone the time of theological silence is irretrievably past.

Even to begin to speak is to question radically some time-honored Midrashic doctrines; and, of these, one is immediately shattered. As we have seen, even the ancient rabbis were forced to suspend the Biblical "for our sins are we punished," perhaps not in response to the destruction of the Temple by Titus, but in response to the paganization of Jerusalem by Hadrian.[17] We too may at most only suspend the Biblical doctrine, if only because we, no more than the rabbis, dare either to deny our own sinfulness or to disconnect it from history. Yet, suspend it we must. For however we twist and turn this doctrine in response to Auschwitz, it becomes a religious absurdity and even a sacrilege. Are "sin" and "retribution" to be given an individual connotation? What a sacrilegious thought when among the Nazis' victims were more than one million children! Are we to give them a collective connotation? What an appalling idea when it was not our Western, agnostic, faithless, and rich but rather the poorest, most pious, and most faithful Jewish communities which were most grievously stricken! As in our torment we turn, as an ultimate resort, to the traditional doctrine that all Israelites of all generations are responsible for each other, we are still totally aghast, for not a single one of the six million died because they had failed to keep the divine-Jewish covenant: they all died because their great-grandparents *had* kept it, if only to the minimum extent of raising Jewish children. Here is the point where we reach radical religious absurdity. Here is the rock on which the "for our sins are we punished" suffers total shipwreck.

Did Jews at Auschwitz die, then, because of the sins of others? The fact, to be sure, is obvious enough, and evidence continues to mount that these others were by no means confined to the Nazi murderers.[18] What is in question, however, is whether a religious meaning can be found in this fact—whether we, like countless generations before us, can have recourse to the thought of martyrdom.

We have already made reference to Abraham's sacrifice of Isaac. The Midrash (which, like the Bible itself, abhors human sacrifice) transfigures the story into one of martyrdom.

Isaac was not a child but rather a grown-up man of thirty-seven years, and he was no unwilling sacrifice but rather a willing martyr—for *Kiddush Hashem*, the sanctification of the divine Name. This Midrashic interpretation continued to be alive in the Jewish religious consciousness, and during the crusades it sustained countless martyrs.[19]

Can it sustain the Jewish religious consciousness after Auschwitz?[20] When the crusading mobs fell upon the Jews of the Rhenish cities of Worms and Mayence (1096 C.E.) they left them, in theory if not in practice, with the choice between death and conversion, thus enabling them to choose martyrdom. At Auschwitz, however, there was no choice; the young and the old, the faithful and the faithless were slaughtered without discrimination. Can there be martyrdom where there is no choice?

Yet we protest against a negative answer, for we protest against allowing Hitler to dictate the terms of our religious life. If not martyrdom, there can be a faithfulness resembling it, when a man has no choice between life and death but only between faith and despair.

But could and did Jews at Auschwitz choose faithfulness unto death? There every effort was made to destroy faith where faith had existed. Torquemada destroyed bodies in order to save souls. Eichmann sought to destroy souls before he destroyed bodies. Throughout the ages pious Jews have died saying the *Shema Yisrael*—"Hear, O Israel, the Lord our God, the Lord is One" (Deut. 6:4). The Nazi murder machine was systematically designed to stifle this *Shema Yisrael* on Jewish lips before it murdered Jews themselves. Auschwitz was the supreme, most diabolical attempt ever made to murder martyrdom itself and, failing that, to deprive all death, martyrdom included, of its dignity.

Hitler and Eichmann have won their victories. A museum in an Israeli kibbutz of death-camp survivors[21] demonstrates that, given the power, determination, machinery, and diabolical cunning, it is possible to murder a nation of heroes. It would, alas, be possible to show that, given these instruments, it is possible to degrade and dehumanize a community of saints. A good Christian suggests that perhaps Auschwitz was a divine reminder of the sufferings of Christ.[22] Should he not ask instead whether his Master himself, had He been present at Auschwitz, could have resisted degradation and dehumanization? What are the sufferings of the Cross compared to those of a mother whose child is slaughtered to the sound of laughter or the strains of a Viennese waltz? This question may sound sacrilegious to Christian ears. Yet we dare not shirk it, for we— Christian as well as Jew—must ask: at Auschwitz, did the grave win the victory after all, or, worse than the grave, did the devil himself win?

Yet we still insist, and this with certain knowledge, that pious Jews *did* die in faithfulness, their faith untouched and unsullied by all the sadism and the horror.[23] Even so, however, Jewish if not Christian[24] exaltation of martyrdom is radically shaken—perhaps forever. The Midrashic Abraham remonstrates with God after the trial is over, for he demands to know its purpose; and he is told that the idolatrous nations, not God Himself, had stood in need of his testimony.[25] The martyrs of Worms and Mayence remembered this Midrash when they saw their children slaughtered before their very eyes, or, worse, themselves laid hands upon them; yet even they must surely have asked themselves whether murder and idolatry had diminished since the times of Abraham, and whether any purpose was served by further Jewish martyrdom. After Auschwitz, however, ours is a far worse question. One would dearly like to believe that the shock of the holocaust has made impossible a second holocaust anywhere. Is the grim truth not rather that a second holocaust has been made more likely, not less likely, by the fact of the first? For there are few signs anywhere of that radical repentance which alone could rid the world of Hitler's shadow.

If this is indeed the grim truth, is not, after Auschwitz, any Jewish willingness to suffer martyrdom, instead of an inspiration to potential saints, much rather an encouragement to potential criminals? After Auschwitz, is not even the saint-

liest Jew driven to the inexorable conclusion that he owes
the moral obligation to the antisemites of the world not to
encourage them by his own powerlessness? Such, at any rate,
is the view of a novelist, himself a survivor, who asserts that the
Warsaw Ghetto uprising and the Eichmann trial have brought
to an end "the millennial epoch of the Jews' sanctifying God
and themselves by their submitting to a violent death."[26]

We turn next to Midrashim of protest. There is a kind
of faith which will accept all things and renounce every protest. There is also a kind of protest which has despaired of
faith. In Judaism there has always been protest which *stays
within* the sphere of faith. Abraham remonstrates with God. So
do Jeremiah and Job. So does, in modern times, the Hasidic
Rabbi Levi Yitzḥak of Berdiczev. He once interrupted the
sacred Yom Kippur service in order to protest that, whereas
kings of flesh and blood protected their peoples, Israel was un-
protected by her King in heaven. Yet having made his protest,
he recited the Kaddish, which begins with these words: "Ex-
tolled and hallowed be the name of God throughout the
world. . . ."

Can Jewish protest today remain within the sphere of
faith? Jeremiah protests against the prosperity of the wicked;
we protest against the slaughter of the innocent. To Job children were restored; that the children of Auschwitz will be
restored is a belief which we dare not abuse for the purpose
of finding comfort. Job protests on his own behalf, and within
the sphere of faith; we protest on behalf of others, and above
all on behalf of those who would not or could not be or stay
within the sphere of Jewish faith and yet were murdered on
account of it. In faithfulness to the victims we must refuse
comfort; and in faithfulness to Judaism we must refuse to disconnect God from the holocaust. Thus, in our case, protest
threatens to escalate into a totally destructive conflict between
the faith of the past and faithfulness to the present.

As we shrink from this conflict we seek refuge in Midrashim of divine powerlessness. However, here too we seem
threatened with ruin. In the Midrash the fear of God still

exists among the nations, and Israel survives, albeit powerless and scattered among the nations.[27] In Nazi Europe, however, the fear of God was dead, and Jews were hunted without mercy or scruple. In the Midrash, God goes into exile with His people and returns with them;[28] from Auschwitz there was no return. Hence, whereas in the Midrash God is only "as it were" powerless, in *Night*, Wiesel sees Him in the face of a child hanging on the gallows.

> One day when we came back from work, we saw three gallows rearing up in the assembly place, three black crows. Roll Call. SS all round us, machine guns trained: the traditional ceremony. Three victims in chains—and one of them, the little servant, the sad-eyed angel.
>
> The SS seemed more preoccupied, more disturbed than usual. To hang a young boy in front of thousands of spectators was no light matter. The head of the camp read the verdict. All eyes were on the child. He was lividly pale, almost calm, biting his lips. The gallows threw its shadow over him. . . .
>
> The three victims mounted together onto the chairs.
>
> The three necks were placed at the same moment within the nooses.
>
> "Long live liberty!" cried the two adults.
>
> But the child was silent.
>
> "Where is God? Where is He?" someone behind me asked.
>
> At a sign from the head of the camp, the three chairs tipped over. . . .
>
> I heard a voice within me answer . . . :
>
> "Where is He? Here He is—He is hanging on this gallows. . . ."[29]

To stake all on divine powerlessness today, therefore, would be to take it both radically and literally. God suffers literal and radical powerlessness, i.e., actual death; and any resurrected divine power will be manifest, not so much within history as beyond it. A Jew, in short, would have to become a Christian. But (as will be seen)[30] never in the two thousand years of Jewish-Christian confrontation has it been less possible for a

Jew to abandon either his Jewishness or his Judaism and embrace Christianity.

Jewish faith thus seems to find no refuge in Midrashim of divine powerlessness, none in otherworldliness, none in the redeeming power of martyrdom, and most of all none in the view that Auschwitz is punishment for the sins of Israel. Unless the God of history is to be abandoned, only a prayer remains, addressed to divine Power, but spoken softly lest it be heard.

One refuge is still unexplored. Rabbi Akiba once taught that God, as it were powerless, shares Israel's exile. It will be recalled that Rabbi Eliezer responded differently to the destruction of the second Temple and the paganization of Jerusalem. The gates of prayer were closed, and only those of tears were still open. Israel was separated from her Father in heaven as by a wall of iron.[31] God was no longer present in history. Was God absent at Auschwitz? Is He in eclipse even now? May pious Jews pray as loudly as they like, because God cannot or does not hear?

We have seen that Buber's image of the eclipse of God can sustain Jewish faith in its confrontation with modern secularism.[32] It now appears, however, that this image fails to sustain us in our confrontation with the Nazi holocaust. Why could Rabbi Eliezer continue to pray when the gates of prayer were closed? Because the divine Presence remained the object of hope, and because for this reason the root experiences of the past could continue to be reenacted. For the hero of Wiesel's *The Gates of the Forest*, however, a Messiah who can come, and yet at Auschwitz did not come, has become an impossibility;[33] and this impossibility, were it to be and remain total and absolute,[34] would be of devastating consequence. A divine eclipse which were *total* in the present would cut off both past and future. The pious Jew during the Passover Seder has always reenacted the salvation at the Red Sea. The event always remained real for him because He who once had saved was saving still.[35] And this latter affirmation could continue to be made, even in times of catastrophe, because the divine salvation remained present in the form of hope. What if our present is without hope? The unprecedented catastrophe of the holocaust now discloses for us that the eclipse of God remains a religious possibility within Judaism only *if it is not total.* If *all present* access to the God of history is wholly lost, the God of history is Himself lost.[36]

With this conclusion we have come face to face with the horrifying possibility mentioned at the beginning—that Hitler has succeeded in murdering, not only one third of the Jewish people, but the Jewish faith as well. Only one response may seem to remain—the cry of total despair—"there is no judgment and no judge."

# Jewish Secularism and the Holocaust

But this conclusion has been reached long ago by the Jewish secularist, albeit for totally different reasons and to a totally different effect.

Jewish secularism has been a possibility ever since the Age of Enlightenment, and its vitality has been confirmed in our time in the most dramatic possible way by the foundation of a secular Jewish state. Today we must ask whether secularism may not be now the common fate of all Jews who persist in their Jewishness. However, we shall find that, if the death camps threaten the Jewish faith, they threaten no less any secularism which would take its place. All religious faith is in crisis in our time. A Jew who confronts Auschwitz and reaffirms his Jewishness discovers that every form of modern secularism is equally in crisis.

We have previously considered the rational grounds for secularism. We must now inquire into the grounds of its attractiveness for modern Jews. The secularism which we have termed subjectivist reductionism dissipates all gods, destroys all meaning except what is humanly created, and deprives

Jewish existence of its millennial distinctiveness. Why should
Jews *want* to—rather than be *rationally compelled* to—accept
such a creed?

Subjectivist reductionism has a general attraction. To the
pious a life without Absolutes may be meaningless and goal-
less. To the secularist such a life is one of liberty. To the
believer the divine Presence exalts as it gives life a focus. To
the secularist it seems to tyrannize, for it stifles life's natural
pluralism for him. The life of faith is abnormal, and the
dissipation of faith ushers in human normalcy. Such is the
creed of the secular city.[37]

If for modern Jews this creed has always had a special
attraction, it is because of the vision of "normalcy" which is
part of it. The modern Jew has become modern by virtue
of the Emancipation, and the Emancipation has been a process of "normalization." Its Gentile donors may have often
had in mind the end of the Jewish people;[38] its Jewish recipients
wished to normalize the Jewish people even when they were
determined to perpetuate it; and, after many centuries of religious discrimination and persecution, this is not surprising.

Nor in view of these many centuries is it surprising that
"Jewish normalcy" has often been not *one limited* goal but
rather *the ultimate* goal. This is true of many "religious" Jews
when they categorize themselves as Jewish by "denomination"
and British, French, or American by "nationality." It is more
true of "secularist" Jews proper when they define themselves
as a "nationality" like all others. Most of all it is true of those
Zionist Jews who, when they embark on the most abnormal
enterprise of restoring a nation after two thousand years, are
committed to the goal of becoming a nation like all others.
The assimilationist has wished all along to solve the so-called
"Jewish problem"[39] by dissolving Jewish existence; the secularist, by depriving it of its millennial distinctiveness.

We cannot guess what might have happened to this modern Jewish secularist or quasi-secularist drive for normalcy had
the Nazi holocaust never occurred. We must face the fact,
however, that had normalcy remained the all-overriding goal,

the Jewish response to the holocaust should have been the exact opposite of the one which actually was and is being given. For twelve long years Jews had been singled out by a hate which was as groundless as it was implacable. For twelve long years a power had held sway in the heart of Europe to which the death of every Jewish man, woman, and child was the one and only unshakable principle. For twelve long years the world had failed to oppose this principle with an equally unshakable principle of its own. Any Jew, then or now, making normalcy his supreme goal should have been, and still should be, in flight from this singled-out condition in total disarray. In fact, however, secularist no less than religious Jews have responded with a reaffirmation of their Jewish existence such as no social scientist would have predicted even if the holocaust had never occurred. Jewish theology still does not know how to respond to Auschwitz. Jews themselves—rich and poor, learned and ignorant, believer and secularist—have responded in some measure all along.

No doubt social scientists have their ready explanations. Persecution stiffens resistence. Humiliation causes pride in half-remembered loyalties. The ancient rabbis themselves suggest that Israel thrives on persecution. Such are the normal explanations, and in normal times they may well be right.

The times, however, are not normal times. A Jew at Auschwitz was not a specimen of the class "victim of prejudice" or even "victim of genocide." He was *singled out* by a demonic power which sought his death *absolutely*, i.e., as an end in itself. For a Jew today merely to affirm his Jewish existence is to accept his singled-out condition; it is to oppose the demons of Auschwitz: and it is to oppose them in the only way in which they can be opposed—with an *absolute* opposition. Moreover, it is to stake on that absolute opposition nothing less than his life and the lives of his children and the lives of his children's children.

The holocaust has thus placed the Jewish secularist into a position for which secularism has no precedent within or without Jewish existence. As a secularist, he views the modern world as a desacralized world from which all gods have vanished. As a Jewish secularist he knows that the devil, if not God, is alive. As a secularist he has relativized all former absolutes. As a Jewish secularist he opposes the demons of Auschwitz absolutely by his mere commitment to Jewish survival. Thus a radical contradiction has appeared in Jewish secularist existence in our time. As secularist the Jewish secularist seeks Jewish normalcy; as Jewish secularist he fragments this normalcy by accepting his singled-out Jewish condition. As secularist, he reduces all absolute to relative affirmations; as Jewish secularist he opposes absolutely the demons of death with his own Jewish life. Throughout the ages the religious Jew was a witness to God. After Auschwitz even the most secularist of Jews bears witness, by the mere affirmation of his Jewishness, against the devil.[40]

The Jewish secularist cannot escape this contradiction; or rather, he could escape it only if he either pretended that the Nazi holocaust had never occurred or else fled from his Jewishness. Will Herberg has therefore rightly asserted that Jewish secularism has become illogical in our time—that, by the logic of his position, the Jewish secularist should abandon his Jewishness.[41] Herberg has failed to notice, however, a truth of far greater consequence which the Jewish secularist himself recognizes: the devil confounds our logic.

Still, not all Jewish secularism falls into immediate contradiction. We have seen that, beside a secularism which dissolves all religious absolutes, there is a secularism which internalizes and transforms these absolutes.[42] Hence a Jewish secularism is conceivable which opposes the demons of Auschwitz absolutely—but in behalf of "free," autonomous, post-religious humanity.

A Jewish secularism of this kind was always problematic. Either the ancient religious absolutes remained absolute in the process of internalization; but then they were universals such as Reason or Progress, and Jewish existence had become accidental. Or else they remained particularized enough to sustain Jewish existence in its particularity; but then they would become idolatrous unless they lost their absoluteness. Jewish romantics and pragmatists both perceived that any specifically "Jewish genius" could be but one instrument in an orchestra requiring many others, and that any Jewish loyalty to Jewish "peoplehood" required by such a genius could exist only within a "pluralistic" scheme in which many loyalties made their respective claims, and in which none was absolute. The God of Judaism—who was and remained other-than-man—could both be Himself universal and single out the Jewish people. The internalized God of secularism could only be either universal (and then not single out at all) or else particular (and then not single out absolutely).

After Auschwitz both alternatives, always problematic within Jewish existence, are fragmented. Jewish opposition to the demons of Auschwitz cannot be understood in terms of humanly created ideals. Those of Reason fail, for Reason is too innocent of demonic evil to fathom the scandal of the particularity of Auschwitz, and too abstractly universal to do justice to the singled-out Jewish condition. The ideals of Progress fail, for Progress makes of Auschwitz at best a throwback into tribalism and at worst a dialectically justified necessity. Least adequate are any ideals which might be furnished by a specifically Jewish genius, for Jewish survival after Auschwitz is not one relative ideal among others but rather an imperative which brooks no compromise. In short, within the context of Jewish existence the secularism which we have termed subjectivist reductionism is breached by absolute Jewish opposition to the demons of Auschwitz; and the secularism which we have seen exemplified in Nietzscheanism and left-wing Hegelianism is breached because internalized absolutes either cannot single out or else cannot remain absolute. Jewish opposition to Auschwitz cannot be grasped in terms of humanly created ideals but only as an imposed commandment. And the Jewish secularist, no less than the believer, is absolutely singled out by a Voice as truly other than man-made ideals—an imperative as truly given—as was the Voice of Sinai.

According to the Midrash, God wished to give the Torah

immediately upon the Exodus from Egypt, but had to postpone the gift until Israel was united.[43] Today, the distinction between religious and secularist Jews is superseded by that between unauthentic Jews who flee from their Jewishness and authentic Jews who affirm it. This latter group includes religious and secularist Jews. These are united by a commanding Voice which speaks from Auschwitz.

## *The Commanding Voice of Auschwitz*

What does the Voice of Auschwitz command?

Jews are forbidden to hand Hitler posthumous victories. They are commanded to survive as Jews, lest the Jewish people perish. They are commanded to remember the victims of Auschwitz lest their memory perish. They are forbidden to despair of man and his world, and to escape into either cynicism or otherworldliness, lest they cooperate in delivering the world over to the forces of Auschwitz. Finally, they are forbidden to despair of the God of Israel, lest Judaism perish. A secularist Jew cannot make himself believe by a mere act of will, nor can he be commanded to do so. . . . And a religious Jew who has stayed with his God may be forced into new, possibly revolutionary relationships with Him. One possibility, however, is wholly unthinkable. A Jew may not respond to Hitler's attempt to destroy Judaism by himself cooperating in its destruction. In ancient times, the unthinkable Jewish sin was idolatry. Today, it is to respond to Hitler by doing his work.[44]

Elie Wiesel has compared the holocaust with Sinai in revelatory significance—and expressed the fear that we are not listening. We shrink from this daring comparison—but even more from not listening. We shrink from any claim to have heard—but even more from a false refuge, in an endless agnosticism, from a Voice speaking to us. I was able to make the above, fragmentary statement (which I have already previously made and here merely quote) only because it no more than articulates what is being heard by Jews the world over— rich and poor, learned and ignorant, believing and secularist. I cannot go beyond this earlier statement but only expand it.

## 1. The First Fragment

In the murder camps the unarmed, decimated, emaciated survivors often rallied their feeble remaining resources for a final, desperate attempt at revolt. The revolt was hopeless. There was no hope but one. One might escape. Why must one escape? To tell the tale. Why must the tale be told when evidence was already at hand that the world would not listen?[45] Because not to tell the tale, when it might be told, was unthinkable. The Nazis were not satisfied with mere murder. Before murdering Jews, they were trying to reduce them to numbers; after murdering them, they were dumping their corpses into nameless ditches or making them into soap. They were making as sure as was possible to wipe out every trace of memory. Millions would be as though they had never been. But to the pitiful and glorious desperadoes of Warsaw, Treblinka, and Auschwitz, who would soon themselves be as though they had never been, not to rescue for memory what could be rescued was unthinkable because it was sacrilege.[46]

It will remain a sacrilege ever after. Today, suggestions come from every side to the effect that the past had best be forgotten, or at least remain unmentioned, or at least be coupled with the greatest and most thoughtless speed with other, but quite different, human tragedies. Sometimes these suggestions come from Jews rationalizing their flight from the Nazi holocaust. More often they come from non-Jews, who rationalize their own flight, or even maintain, affrontingly enough, that unless Jews universalize the holocaust, thus robbing the Jews of Auschwitz of their Jewish identity, they are guilty of disregard for humanity.[47] But for a Jew hearing the commanding Voice of Auschwitz the duty to remember and to tell the tale, is not negotiable. It is holy. The religious Jew still possesses this word. The secularist Jew is commanded to restore it. A secular holiness, as it were, has forced itself into his vocabulary.

## 2. The Second Fragment

Jewish survival, were it even for no more than survival's sake, is a holy duty as well. The murderers of Auschwitz cut off Jews from humanity and denied them the right to existence; yet in being denied that right, Jews represented all humanity. Jews after Auschwitz represent all humanity when they affirm their Jewishness and deny the Nazi denial. They would fail if they affirmed the mere *right* to their Jewishness, participating, as it were, in an obscene debate between others who deny the right of Jews to exist and Jews who affirm it.[48] Nor would they deny the Nazi denial if they affirmed merely their humanity-in-general, permitting an antisemitic split between their humanity and their Jewishness, or, worse, agreeing to vanish as Jews in one way, in response to Hitler's attempt to make them vanish in another. The commanding Voice of Auschwitz singles Jews out; Jewish survival is a commandment which brooks no compromise. It was this Voice which was heard by the Jews of Israel in May and June 1967 when they refused to lie down and be slaughtered.[49]

Yet such is the extent of Hitler's posthumous victories that Jews, commanded to survive as Jews, are widely denied even the right. More precisely—for overt antisemitism is not popular in the post-holocaust world—they are granted the right only on certain conditions. Russians, Poles, Indians, and Arabs have a natural right to exist; Jews must earn that right. Other states must refrain from wars of aggression; the State of Israel is an "aggressor" even if it fights for its life. Peoples unscarred by Auschwitz ought to protest when any evil resembling Auschwitz is in sight, such as the black ghettoes or Vietnam. The Jewish survivors of Auschwitz have no right to survive unless they engage in such protests. Other peoples may include secularists and believers. Jews must be divided

into bad secularists or Zionists, and good—albeit anachronistic
—saints who stay on the cross.

The commanding Voice of Auschwitz bids Jews reject all
such views as a monumental affront. It bids them reject as no
longer tolerable every version—Christian or leftist, Gentile or
Jewish—of the view that the Jewish people is an anachronism,
when it is the elements of the world perpetrating and permitting Auschwitz, not its survivors, that are anachronistic. A
Jew is commanded to descend from the cross and, in so doing,
not only to reiterate his ancient rejection of an ancient Christian view but also to suspend the time-honored Jewish exaltation of martyrdom. For after Auschwitz, Jewish life is more
sacred than Jewish death, were it even for the sanctification of
the divine Name. The left-wing secularist Israeli journalist
Amos Kenan writes: "After the death camps, we are left only
one supreme value: existence."[50]

## 3. The Third Fragment

But such as Kenan, being committed and unrepentant
lovers of the downtrodden, accept other supreme values as
well, and will suspend these only when Jewish existence itself
is threatened or denied. Kenan has a universal vision of peace,
justice, and brotherhood. He loves the poor of Cuba and hates
death in Vietnam. In these and other commitments such left-
wing secularists share the ancient Jewish religious, messianical-
ly inspired refusal to embrace either pagan cynicism (which
despairs of the world and accepts the *status quo*) or Christian
or pseudo-Christian otherworldliness (which despairs of the
world and flees from it). The commanding Voice of Auschwitz
bids Jews, religious and secularist, not to abandon the world
to the forces of Auschwitz, but rather to continue to
work and hope for it. Two possibilities are equally ruled out:
to despair of the world on account of Auschwitz, abandoning
the age-old Jewish identification with poor and persecuted
humanity; and to abuse such identification as a means of flight
from Jewish destiny. It is precisely *because* of the uniqueness
of Auschwitz, and *in* his Jewish particularity, that a Jew must

be at one with humanity. For it is precisely because Auschwitz
has made the world a desperate place that a Jew is forbidden
to despair of it.[51] The hero of Wiesel's *The Gates of the Forest*
asserts that it is too late for the Messiah—and that for exactly
this reason we are commanded to hope.[52]

## 4. The Fourth Fragment

The Voice of Auschwitz commands the religious Jew after
Auschwitz to continue to wrestle with his God in however
revolutionary ways; and it forbids the secularist Jew (who has
already, and on other grounds, lost Him) to use Auschwitz as
an additional weapon wherewith to deny Him.

The ways of the religious Jew are revolutionary, for there
is no previous Jewish protest against divine Power like his
protest. Continuing to hear the Voice of Sinai as he hears
the Voice of Auschwitz, his citing of God against God may
have to assume extremes which dwarf those of Abraham,
Jeremiah, Job, Rabbi Levi Yitzḥak. (You have abandoned the
covenant? We shall not abandon it! You no longer want Jews
to survive? We shall survive, as better, more faithful, more
pious Jews! You have destroyed all grounds for hope? We
shall obey the commandment to hope which You Yourself
have given!) Nor is there any previous Jewish compassion with
divine powerlessness like the compassion required by such a
powerlessness. (The fear of God is dead among the nations?
We shall keep it alive and be its witnesses! The times are
too late for the coming of the Messiah? We shall persist without hope and recreate hope—and, as it were, divine Power—by
our persistence!) For the religious Jew, who remains within
the Midrashic framework, the Voice of Auschwitz manifests
a divine Presence which, as it were, is shorn of all except commanding Power. This Power, however, is inescapable.

No less inescapable is this Power for the secularist Jew
who has all along been outside the Midrashic framework and
this despite the fact that the Voice of Auschwitz does not
enable him to return into that framework. He cannot return;
but neither may he turn the Voice of Auschwitz against that

of Sinai. For he may not cut off his secular present from the
religious past: the Voice of Auschwitz commands preservation
of that past. Nor may he widen the chasm between himself
and the religious Jew: the Voice of Auschwitz commands
Jewish unity.

As religious and secularist Jews are united in kinship with
all the victims of Auschwitz and against all the executioners,
they face a many-sided mystery and find a simple certainty. As
regards the minds and souls of the victims of Auschwitz, God's
presence to them is a many-sided mystery which will never
be exhausted either by subsequent committed believers or by
subsequent committed unbelievers, and least of all by subsequent neutral theorists—psychological, sociological, philosophical, theological—who spin out their theories immune to love
and hate, submission and rage, faith and despair. As regards
the murderers of Auschwitz, however, there was no mystery,
for they denied, mocked, murdered the God of Israel six million times—and together with Him four thousand years of
Jewish faith. For a Jew after Auschwitz, only one thing is certain: he may not side with the murderers and do what they
have left undone. The religious Jew who has heard the Voice
of Sinai must continue to listen as he hears the commanding
Voice of Auschwitz. And the secularist Jew, who has all along
lost Sinai and now hears the Voice of Auschwitz, cannot abuse
that Voice as a means to destroy four thousand years of Jewish
believing testimony. The rabbis assert that the first Temple
was destroyed because of idolatry. Jews may not destroy the
Temple which is the tears of Auschwitz by doing, wittingly or
unwittingly, Hitler's work.

## 5. The Clash Between the Fragments

Such is the commanding Voice of Auschwitz as it is
increasingly being heard by Jews of this generation. But how
can it be obeyed? Each of the four fragments described—and
they are mere fragments, and the description has been poor
and inadequate—is by itself overwhelming. Taken together,

they seem unbearable. For there are clashes between them which tear us apart.

How can the religious Jew be faithful to both the faith of the past and the victims of the present? We have already asked this question, but are now further from an answer than before. For a reconciliation by means of willing martyrdom is ruled out by the duty to Jewish survival, and a reconciliation by means of refuge in otherworldly mysticism is ruled out by the duty to hold fast to the world and to continue to hope and work for it. God, world and Israel are in so total a conflict when they meet at Auschwitz as to seem to leave religious Jews confronting that conflict with nothing but a prayer addressed to God, yet spoken softly lest it be heard: in short, with madness.

But the conflict is no less unbearable for the secularist Jew. To be sure, the space once occupied by God is void for him or else occupied by a question mark. Only three of the four fragments effectively remain. Yet the conflict which remains tears him asunder.

Søren Kierkegaard's "knight of faith" was obliged to retrace the road which led Abraham to Mount Moriah, where Isaac's sacrifice was to take place.[53] A Jew today is obliged to retrace the road which led his brethren to Auschwitz. It is a road of pain and mourning, of humiliation, guilt, and despair. To retrace it is living death. How suffer this death and also choose Jewish life which, like all life, must include joy, laughter, and childlike innocence? How reconcile such a remembrance with life itself? How dare a Jewish parent crush his child's innocence with the knowledge that his uncle or grandfather was denied life because of his Jewishness? And how dare he not burden him with this knowledge? The conflict is inescapable, for we may neither forget the past for the sake of present life, nor destroy present life by a mourning without relief—and there is no relief.

Nor is this all. The first two fragments above clash with each other: each clashes with the third as well. No Jewish secularist today may continue to hope and work for mankind as though Auschwitz had never happened, falling back on secularist beliefs of yesterday that man is good, progress real, and brotherhood inevitable. Yet neither may he, on account of Auschwitz, despair of human brotherhood and cease to hope and work for it. How face Auschwitz and not despair? How hope and work, and not act as though Auschwitz had never occurred? Yet to forget and to despair are both forbidden.

Perhaps reconciliation would be possible if the Jewish secularist of today, like the Trotskys and Rosa Luxemburgs of yesterday, could sacrifice Jewish existence on the altar of future humanity. (Is this in the minds of "progressive" Jews when they protest against war in Vietnam but refuse to protest against Polish antisemitism? Or in the minds of what Kenan calls the "good people" of the world when they demand that Israel hand over weapons to those sworn to destroy her?) This sacrifice, however, is forbidden, and the altar is false. The left-wing Israeli secularist Kenan may accept all sorts of advice from his progressive friends, but not that he allow himself to be shot for the good of humanity. Perhaps he has listened for a moment even to this advice, for he hates a gun in his hand. Perhaps he has even wished for a second he could accept it, feeling, like many of his pious ancestors, that it is better to be killed than to kill. Yet he firmly rejects such advice, for he is commanded to reject it; rather than be shot, he will shoot first when there is no third alternative. But he will shoot with tears in his eyes. He writes:

> Why weren't the June 4 borders peace borders on the fourth of June, but will only become so now? Why weren't the UN Partition Plan borders of 1947 peace borders then, but will become so now? Why should I return his gun to the bandit as a reward for having failed to kill me?
>
> I want peace peace peace peace, peace peace peace.
>
> I am ready to give everything back in exchange for peace. And I shall give nothing back without peace.
>
> I am ready to solve the refugee problem. I am ready to accept an independent Palestinian state. I am ready to

sit and talk. About everything, all at the same time. Direct talks, indirect talks, all this is immaterial. But peace.

Until you agree to have peace, I shall give back nothing. And if you force me to become a conqueror, I shall become a conqueror. And if you force me to become an oppressor, I shall become an oppressor. And if you force me into the same camp with all the forces of darkness in the world, there I shall be.[54]

Kenan's article ends:

. . . if I survive . . . , without a god but without prophets either, my life will have no sense whatever. I shall have nothing else to do but walk on the banks of streams, or on the top of the rocks, watch the wonders of nature, and console myself with the words of Ecclesiastes, the wisest of men: For the light is sweet, and it is good for the eyes to see the sun.[55]

The conclusion, then, is inescapable. Secularist Jewish existence after Auschwitz is threatened with a madness no less extreme than that which produces a prayer addressed to God, yet spoken softly lest it be heard.

# Madness and the Commanding Voice of Auschwitz

The Voice of Auschwitz commands Jews not to go mad. It commands them to accept their singled out condition, face up to its contradictions, and endure them. Moreover, it gives the power of endurance, the power of sanity. The Jew of today can endure because he must endure, and he must endure because he is commanded to endure.

We ask: whence has come our strength to endure even these twenty-five years—not to flee or disintegrate but rather to stay, however feebly, at our solitary post, to affirm, however weakly, our Jewishness, and to bear witness, if only by this affirmation, against the forces of hell itself? The question produces abiding wonder. It is at a commanding Voice without which we, like the Psalmist (Ps. 119:92), would have perished in our affliction.

## Witness Unto the Nations

When the Israelite maidservants at the Red Sea and Mount Sinai saw what neither Isaiah nor Ezekiel nor all the other prophets were to see, they found themselves to be, to their own radical astonishment, witnesses unto the nations. Had this been otherwise, their astonishment at the divine Presence would have been itself neither radical nor abiding. The divine saving Presence at the Red Sea was sole Power: hence it required recognition of all the nations and promised salvation for all the nations. The divine commanding Presence at Mount Sinai too was sole Power: hence it required action of all human creatures and promised a covenant with all human creatures. Yet, the divine Presence was fragmentary and occurred in history: hence it did not dissolve Israel into the nations but rather made her a singled out witness unto the nations.

This fact of being a witness was never questioned throughout the millennia of the Jewish faith. Yet the nature of the required testimony was prey to recurring puzzlement with the change of historical circumstances. Thus in Biblical times the testimony was against idolatry; yet it was clear even then that not all Gentiles were idolaters. As for the rabbis, they formed a firm concept of a divine covenant with the children of Noah, as well as of "righteous Gentiles" among the nations, who required neither conversion to Judaism nor instruction in it in their achievement of righteousness. What then was the nature of the required testimony?

At times it could seem to be between God, Israel and the nations. This was true, negatively, of the testimony against idolatry. It was true, positively, of the testimony to the One

God which led to Christian and Muhammadan monotheism. It could be accepted as true also when in modern times Jews invoked their faith in partial or total support of social progress and secularist Messianism. It could seem true even when Jewish martyrs recalled the Midrashic account of Isaac's sacrifice, persisting in the belief that Jewish martyrdom had an effect on the world.

At other times, however, Jewish testimony, albeit to the nations, was between God and Israel alone, if only because to hold otherwise would have led to despair. Thus the Jews behind medieval ghetto walls could not seriously believe that the nations on the other side knew or cared about their faithfulness or faithlessness to the Torah; nor could the martyrs of Worms and Mayence seriously think that the crusading mobs would be moved by their martyrdom. And while it is a documented fact that countless pious Jews died at Auschwitz with the *Shema Yisrael* on their lips, no less documented is the fact that, while the Nazi murder machines on occasion broke down, the murderers themselves did not.[56] Nor, to judge by contemporary historians, novelists, philosophers, and theologians, does it seem that the world cares even now.

Even so, pious Jews believed themselves to be witnesses unto the nations. In the medieval ghettoes they believed that by studying the Torah they helped preserve the whole world, since if it were not for the Torah, the world would again become "without form and void" (Gen. 1:2)[57] The martyrs of Worms and Mayence continued to hold fast to the Midrashic Abraham whose sacrifice had been needed not by God but by the world. But what, in their final moments, the pious Jews of Auschwitz believed or did not believe is a mystery which can only be revered but which will never be fathomed.

After Auschwitz does a Jew remain a witness unto the nations, and, if so, what is his testimony? Even the first of these questions is fraught with peril. We shrink from an affirmative answer lest we stifle impulses for sheer survival and elementary normalcy with unnecessary or impossible burdens. Yet we shrink even more from a negative answer lest we cut off any part of the Jewish past, break up kinships of the present, or deny or obscure the universal significance of contemporary Jewish destiny.

What, then, when we hardly dare answer the first question, may be said of the second? The world which is a desperate place for the Jew after Auschwitz is becoming increasingly desperate for all men. Hope is being overwhelmed by despair; love by hate; commandment by loss of direction; and never far below consciousness is the spectre of a nuclear holocaust —the universal Auschwitz. This is an age in which former believers seek refuge in secularity, even as formerly self-confident secularists seek old or new gods. The only universal seems to be an apparent unwillingness or incapacity to endure through the present worldwide crisis; to cherish and nurture what needs to be saved as the foundations are shaking; to work and hope with unyielding stubbornness for a time when our present crisis may have passed, and a new, possibly post-"religious" and post-"secular" age may come in sight.

The Jew after Auschwitz is a witness to endurance. He is singled out by contradictions which, in our post-holocaust world, are worldwide contradictions. He bears witness that without endurance we shall all perish. He bears witness that we can endure because we must endure; and that we must endure because we are commanded to endure.

## Longing, Defiance, Endurance

Can the miracle at the Red Sea still be reenacted? Can the religious Jew still recall it twice daily in his prayers? After Auschwitz can we continue to celebrate the Passover Seder?

How can even the secularist, who has long abandoned the celebration, not reinstate it? When at Jerusalem in 1967 the threat of total annihilation gave way to sudden salvation it was because of Auschwitz, not in spite of it, that there was an abiding astonishment. Nothing of the past was explained or adjusted, no fears for the future were stilled. Yet the very

clash between Auschwitz and Jerusalem produced a moment
of truth—a wonder at a singled out, millennial existence which,
after Auschwitz, is still possible and actual.

But the ancient Passover has acquired a new quality. Always mixed with longing, the celebration is after Auschwitz
mingled with defiance as well. There has always been the
longing for a future when salvation would no longer be fragmentary, when the angels need no longer refrain from sing-
ing, when men everywhere, at last reconciled, would see what
once the Israelite maidservants saw. Astonishingly, this longing survived even at Auschwitz itself. We dare not destroy it
but must keep it alive. A prayer of remembrance, added by
Jews throughout the world to the Passover service, reads as
follows:

> On this night of the Seder we remember with reverence
> and love the six millions of our people of the European
> exile who perished at the hands of a tyrant more wicked
> than the Pharaoh who enslaved our fathers in Egypt.
> Come, said he to his minions, let us cut them off from
> being a people, that the name of Israel may be remem-
> bered no more. And they slew the blameless and the
> pure, men, women and little ones, with vapors of poison
> and burned them with fire. But we abstain from dwelling
> on the deeds of the evil ones lest we defame the image
> of God in which man was created.

> Now, the remnants of our people who were left in the
> ghettos and camps of annihilation rose up against the
> wicked ones for the sanctification of the Name, and slew
> many of them before they died. On the first day of Pass-
> over the remnants of the Ghetto of Warsaw rose up
> against the adversary, even as in the days of Judah the
> Maccabee. They were lovely and pleasant in their lives,
> and in their death they were not divided, and they
> brought redemption to the name of Israel through all
> the world.

> And from the depth of their affliction the martyrs lifted
> their voices in a song of faith in the coming of the

Messiah, when justice and brotherhood will reign among men:

"Ani ma'amin b'emunah sh'lemah b'viat ha-mashiaḥ, v'af al pi sh'yi-tmahmeah im kol ze ani ma'amin"

"I believe with perfect faith in the coming of the Messiah, and though he tarry, nevertheless I believe."

Maimonides, the author of this statement of faith and the wisest of Jewish philosophers, had included the words "though he tarry," knowing they would be necessary.[58] We ask how at Auschwitz, even with these words, this statement of faith remained possible. We shall never know. We do know that the age-old Jewish longing had become mingled with a new defiance and that only thus was there endurance. The old song of longing and hope had become united with a new song of defiance in the midst of hopelessness[59]—the song of the Warsaw Ghetto Jewish Underground:

Dos lid geshribn iz mit blut un nit mit blay
S'iz nit kayn lidl fun a foygl oyf der fray;
Dos hot a folk ts'vishn falndike went
Dos lid gezungen mit naganes in di hent.

Zog nit keynmol az du geyst dem letstn veg
Chotsh himlen blayene farshsteln bloye teg
Kumen vet noch undzer oysgebenkte sho
S'vet a poyk ton undzer trot: mir zeinen do.

This song is written not with lead but with blood,
It is not the song of birds upon the wing
But of a people upon whom the walls came crashing down
Who sang it, weapon in hand.

Do not ever say you go the last road.
Leaden skies may hide the blue day.
Yet the hour we have longed for will arrive.
Our footsteps confirm: we are here.

"Mir zeinen do"—we are here, exist, survive, endure, witnesses to God and man even if abandoned by God and man. Jews after Auschwitz will never understand the longing, defiance, endurance of the Jews at Auschwitz. But so far as is humanly possible they must make them their own as they carry the whole Jewish past forward into a future yet unknown.


NOTES

1. William Hamilton's "The New Optimism—From Prufrock to Ringo" takes a consciously Judaic stance when it sides with Saul Bellow against T. S. Eliot:

> Saul Bellow recently has written about the end of pessimism, and he has significantly spoken of the end of the Wasteland era, the end of the hollow men. Moses Herzog, in Bellow's novel, single-handedly takes on the whole fashionable pessimism of modern intellectual life. He lashes out against those who tell you how good dread is for you; he speaks of the "commonplaces of the Wasteland outlook, the cheap mental stimulants of Alienation, the cant and rant of pipsqueaks about Inauthenticity and Forlornness." Perhaps the most thoroughly post-modern, post-pessimistic act Herzog commits is his decision, at the close of the novel, not to go mad—his decision for human happiness (p. 159).

However, Hamilton's optimism is only pseudo-Judaic, for it is in the end concerned, not with the world, but only with an optimistic attitude toward the world.

> This is not an optimism of grace, but a worldly optimism. . . . It faces despair not with the conviction that out of it God can bring hope, but with the conviction that the human conditions that created it can be overcome, whether those conditions be poverty, discrimination, or mental illness. It faces death not with the hope for immortality, but with the human confidence that man may befriend death and live with it as a possibility always alongside. I think that the new optimism is both a cause and a consequence of the basic theological experience which we today call the death of God (p. 169). (Both excerpts from Radical Theology and the Death of God, copyright © 1966, by Thomas T. J. Altizer and William Hamilton, reprinted by permission of the publishers, The Bobbs-Merrill Company, Inc.)

Absorbed as he is by the conflict between theological "pessimism" and secular "optimism," Hamilton shows no signs of the kind of realism vis-à-vis the dark places of the contemporary world which is as necessary for a "worldly" optimism as for one of "grace." Can the holocaust be classified with poverty, discrimination, or mental illness? Can one "befriend" death at Auschwitz or Hiroshima? So long as questions such as these are not asked the "decision not to go mad" is a cheap decision, and Eliot's spiritualizing "pessimism" is opposed by nothing better than a spiritualizing "optimism." The dread of Auschwitz is assuredly not "good for you"; yet to avoid it for this reason remains a form of unworldly escapism no matter how loudly it proclaims its worldliness.

2. A more precise identification would depend on whether A. Roy Eckhardt is right when he includes the words italicized by us in his definition of Christianity: "The acceptance, through the Holy Spirit, of Jesus as Messiah means beholding him as the one who transforms *and will transform* the world." (*Elder and Younger Brothers* [New York: Scribners, 1967], p. 107.)

3. See above, p. 51.

4. The poet Hölderlin laments that the gods have fled, referring to the Greek gods who were nothing if not pesent in the world and asserting the impossibility of finding them in the modern world. Heidegger takes up Hölderlin's theme.

5. I put "racial" antisemitism into quotation marks to indicate that it is pseudo-racial only, from the standpoint of both the persecutors and the persecuted. With the latter aspect I shall deal subsequently. As regards the former, it must here suffice that my point is not the obvious one that the "racial science" which such antisemitism may invoke is pseudo-science, but rather that it focuses its energies on the fact that whereas one becomes a Christian through baptism one becomes a Jew through birth and, unlike Christian antisemitism, denies that a Jew is redeemable through baptism.

6.

> Over the centuries Christians have generally lived with the tacit assumption that a "good Jew" is either a dead Jew or a Christian. So, alternately, they have consented to the death of Jews and prayed for their conversion. . . . Christians have never really said that God loves the Jew for what he is now. (Quoted by Eckhardt, *op. cit.*, p. 171.)

Eckhardt does not give the reference to the issue of the *Christian Century* in which Rylaarsdam's article originally appeared.

7. The connection is not merely theoretical. Nazi "racial" antisemitism could certainly never have arisen except for a long history of "religious" antisemitism. Moreover (as is only to be expected), "religious" antisemitism did not always stay within the bounds erected by theological theory. Thus in 1298 the Jews of the German town of Röttingen were charged with profanation of the Host. The charge produced a massacre, not only of the Jews of that particular town, but also of those of countless other towns whom no one had even charged with any connection with the supposed crime. Leon Poliakov writes:

> What is new about the incident is that for the first time *all* the Jews of the country were held responsible for a crime imputed to

one or at most several Jews. It is quite likely that as usual the accusation was a pretext for large-scale pillaging. But heretofore incidents of this nature, numerous as they were, had remained in a sense localized. This one spread, and we may say in modern terms that apart from the excesses of the Crusaders it was the first case of Jewish "genocide" in Christian Europe. (*The History of Anti-semitism*, I [New York: Vanguard, 1965], 100.)

8. See especially Norman Cohn, *Warrant For Genocide* (London: Eyre and Spottiswoode, 1967), a work which thoroughly refutes the idea that pre-Hitler Germany—and Europe—is guiltless of all connection with Auschwitz.

9. Jerry Farber, in an article entitled "The Student as Nigger." This article was widely reprinted in student newspapers throughout North America.

10. I have dealt more fully with the uniqueness of the Nazi holocaust in "Jewish Faith and the Holocaust," *Commentary*, 1967. (See also *Quest For Past and Future*, pp. 17 ff.) I feel constrained to stress once again that I assert only that the Nazi genocide of European Jews is unique, not that it is a greater or more tragic crime than all others. Thus, for example, the fate of the Gypsies at the hand of the Nazis (itself an "ideological" project) is at least in one sense more tragic—that no one seems to bother to commemorate them. Even this example of genocide, however, though itself a product of Nazi ideology, still differs from the Nazi genocide of European Jewry: no comparable hate propaganda was directed by the Nazis against the Gypsies. Whence this groundless, infinite hate, indiscriminately directed against adults and children, saints and sinners, and so relentlessly expressed in action?

11. I have quoted the preceding paragraph almost verbatim from the article cited in note 10. What is said in this passage is crucial, and I am unable to express it better now than in my earlier statement.

12. I put "Jewish question" or "problem" into quotation marks to indicate that the question or problem is created by antisemitism and does not exist where there is no antisemitism.

13. See "The State of Jewish Belief: A Symposium," *Commentary* (August 1966), pp. 71–160; reprinted as *The Condition of Jewish Belief* (New York: Macmillan, 1966).

14. See R. L. Rubenstein, "Homeland and Holocaust," *The Religious Situation 1968* (Boston: Beacon, 1968), p. 110.

15. *Op. cit.*, p. 57.

16. . . . *than a Tear in the Sea* (Bergen Belsen Memorial Press, 1967), p. vii.

17. See above, pp. 26 ff.

18. See most recently A. D. Morse, *While Six Million Died* (New York: Random House, 1967).

19. For this Midrash and its medieval use see Shalom Spiegel,

*The Last Trial* (New York: Pantheon, 1967). Spiegel shows the element of protest among the medieval chroniclers which is prominent above all because, while Isaac had been reprieved, no reprieve had occurred for the many Isaacs during the Crusades.

20. We say "after" and not "at" Auschwitz because any opinion as to what was or was not religiously possible at Auschwitz itself is ultimately permissible, if for anyone, only for an actual survivor.

21. *Kibbutz Lohamay Ha-getaot.*

22. In the article cited in note 10, I have already characterized this attempt to find a purpose in Auschwitz as reflecting "a moving sense of desperation, and an incredible lapse of theological judgment." Since the passage I criticize was part of a sermon which was not published but only mimeographed and privately distributed, I feel obliged to withhold the name of the well-known author.

23. Secularist Jews, too, died with Jewish faithfulness; but we are not presently concerned with Jewish secularism.

24. See note 25.

25. This contrasts with Søren Kierkegaard's *Fear and Trembling,* in which God needs to have Abraham's testimony and Abraham needs to give it. Whether Christian (like Jewish) resort to martyrdom is decisively affected by Auschwitz depends on whether worldly effectiveness, however remote or improbable, is part of its meaning, Kierkegaard to the contrary notwithstanding.

26. Manès Sperber, *op. cit.,* p. xiv. I am constrained to quote this remarkable passage in full:

> Genocide, whatever its extent, never succeeds completely. That perpetrated by the Nazis failed more than any other, because it provided the main reasons for the creation of the State of Israel. Encouraged by the way Hitler had practiced genocide without encountering resistance, the Arabs surged in upon the nascent Israeli nation to exterminate it and make themselves its immediate heirs. The military and political leaders of the Arab states, along with Foreign Minister Bevin and his advisers in the Colonial Office, did not understand that the *millennial epoch* of the Jews' sanctifying of God and themselves by their submitting to violent death *had just come to an end with the Warsaw Ghetto* uprising. With this conclusive experience of European Jewry there also came to an end the illusion that they could count on other men to defend them. The Arab armies were cut to pieces and thrown beyond the borders by men who, in going to battle with no thought of retreat, meant also to avenge a people murdered and not buried, whose brothers, sons or nephews they were. They meant to teach the world that the long hunting season was over forever, and that one could no longer kill Jews easily or with impunity. To be sure, the soldiers of this new Hebrew army, Zionists for the most part, were fighting for the land that their labor had redeemed, for the villages, towns and kibbutzim that they had brought into being out of nothingness,

and for the lives of all of them. But they were fighting above all—particularly since 1945 and beyond the spring of 1948—to deliver their people from a degradation that threatened to encourage exterminators, their sons and their grandsons, as well as their innumerable silent accomplices the world over.

For the greatest boon that can be brought to peoples tempted by aggressive anti-Semitism is to make the crime that it inspires dangerous for the instigators and executors themselves. Between 1933 and 1945, the whole world provided Hitler—who moved only step-by-step at first—with proof that he could undertake anything he pleased against the Jews, with nothing to fear but verbal protestations never followed up with the slightest reprisal. This is why the abduction of Eichmann by agents of the State of Israel and his trial in Jerusalem are events of *major significance* (pp. xiii-xiv).

The less than ten pages of which this passage is part were written in 1964; Sperber states that it took him weeks to write them, "every time escaping anew from the shadows of a past whose memory threatens the present" (p. xvi).

27. See above, p. 29.

28. See above, p. 28.

29. Elie Wiesel, *Night* (New York: Pyramid Books, 1961), p. 78.

30. Only briefly and indirectly, since Jewish-Christian relations after the holocaust are not part of my concern in this discourse. (See the article cited in note 10). I here merely wish to state my conviction that the holocaust calls for a new dimension in Jewish-Christian relations—one which cannot be reached until the subject is confronted.

31. See above, pp. 27 ff.

32. See above, pp. 49, 61.

33. *The Gates of the Forest* (New York: Holt, Rinehart and Winston, 1966), p. 225.

34. For Wiesel on this question, see below, p. 88.

35. See above, ch. 1, note 13.

36. Buber himself sees this with the utmost clarity. See the weighty passage quoted at the end of the preceding chapter.

37. To have caught the mood of this creed is the greatest accomplishment of Harvey Cox's *The Secular City* (New York: Macmillan, 1965).

38. Kant expected the "euthanasia" of Judaism. His intentions at the time were benevolent; but today the very phrase sounds obscene.

39. See above, note 12.

40. For my interpretation of Nazism as the supreme and unsurpassable modern idolatry, see "Idolatry as a Modern Religious Possibility," *The Religious Situation 1968* (Boston: Beacon, 1968), pp. 254–87.

41. In a public address heard by the author.

42. See above, pp. 49 ff.

43. *Midrash Tanḥuma*, ed. Buber (Wilma, 1885), Yitro, 37b.

44. Once again I quote from the article cited in note 10, for the reason stated in note 11.

45. See especially Elie Wiesel, "A Plea for the Dead," *Legends of Our Time* (Holt, Rinehart and Winston, 1968), pp. 174–97.

46. See especially Yuri Suhl, *They Fought Back* (New York: Crown, 1967).

47. Wiesel is dismayed to discover that some critics of Nelly Sachs's poetry try to minimize its Jewishness and contrast a "universal vision" with a merely Jewish one. He comments:

> Her greatness lies in her Jewishness, and this makes it belong to all mankind. It is perhaps only natural that there are those who try to remove her, if not to estrange her, from us. But this will never happen. She has many Jewish melodies left to sing. . . . What disturbs me is that strangers have stolen them. ("Conversation With Nelly Sachs," *Jewish Heritage* [Spring 1968], p. 33.)

48. In recent years some North American TV stations and university groups have seen fit to furnish American Nazis and German neo-Nazis with a forum, and even invited Jews to debate with them, apparently utterly oblivious to the obscenity of such invitations.

49. See a letter by Professor Harold Fisch of Bar Ilan University quoted in the article cited in note 10, and also note 26

50. "A Letter to All Good People—To Fidel Castro, Sartre, Russell and All the Rest," *Midstream*, October 1968 (This article originally appeared first in *Yediot Aharonot* and was republished in *The New Statesman*). Here and in the following, I single out this article, not only because of its excellence, but also (a fact doubtless largely accounting for this excellence) because its author is a left-wing secularist (who cannot and will not abandon his universalistic ideals) and an Israeli (who cannot and will not condone collective Jewish suicide).

51. I distinguish with the utmost sharpness between (a) the view that because of Auschwitz the justification of Jewish existence depends on Jews behaving like superhuman saints toward all other peoples ever after and (b) the view that because of Auschwitz Jews are obligated to (i) Jewish survival as an end which, less than ever, needs any justification (ii) work for oppressed and suffering humanity everywhere. I accept the second view, and (as will be seen) the inevitably painful conflicts that go with it. The first view is totally unacceptable.

52. P. 225. See above, p. 78 and note 33.

53. See *Fear and Trembling* (Garden City, N. Y.: Anchor, 1954).

54. *Op. cit.*, p. 35.

55. *Op. cit.*, p. 36.

56. Simon Wiesenthal writes:

> Once Himmler was present when experiments using the exhaust gases of submarine engines for extermination had proved highly unsatisfactory. Himmler had been furious, and there had been drastic punishment. Machines broke down, but the people handling them never did. How could it be that the people operating the gas chambers and ovens were more reliable than the machines? (*The Murderers Among Us* [New York: McGraw-Hill, 1967], p. 315.)

Wiesenthal's revelations about Nazi schools for mass murder give a partial answer to the question.

57. *Midrash Deut. Rabbah*, Nizzabim, VIII, 5.

58. This passage is the twelfth of Maimonides' thirteen principles of Jewish faith.

59. Manès Sperber states that it was not hope but rather despair that inspired the Warsaw Ghetto uprising, and quotes the non-Jewish Polish writer Tadeusz Borowski, an inmate of Auschwitz who committed suicide at the age of twenty-nine:

> It is hope that provokes men to march indifferently to the gas-chambers, and keeps them from conceiving of an insurrection. . . . Never has hope provoked so much ill as in this war, as in this camp. We were never taught to rid ourselves of hope, and that is why we are dying in the gas-chambers (op. cit., pp. xi, xiii).

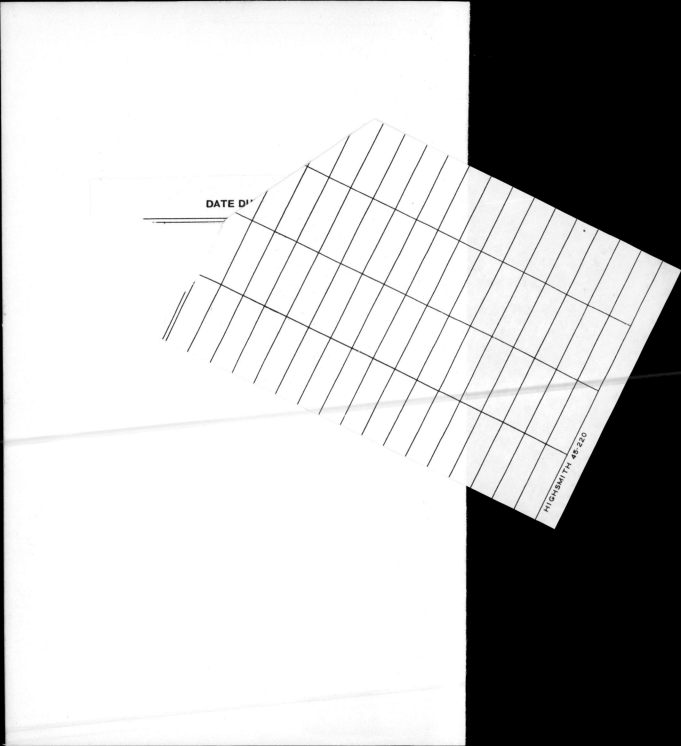

**DATE DU**

HIGHSMITH 45-220